QUEEN VICTORIA IN CORNWALL

✷ ✷ ✷

THE ROYAL VISIT TO CORNWALL IN 1846

Susan Symons

SUSAN SYMONS

Published by Roseland Books
The Old Rectory, St Just-in-Roseland, Truro, Cornwall, TR2 5JD
www.susansymons.com

ISBN: 978-1-8383845-1-7

For Shirley, who loves Cornwall.
With thanks for thirty years of friendship to Mum and me.

CONTENTS

1. Introduction   1

2. The royal yacht Victoria and Albert   11

3. The royal visit day by day   19

4. Cotehele and Mount Edgcumbe   39

5. St Michael's Mount and Kynance Cove   61

6. Pendennis Castle Falmouth and St Mawes Castle   77

7. Restormel Castle and Place House Fowey   93

8. Return to Osborne House   109

9. The duchy of Cornwall and its royal dukes   117

Sketch maps   129

Charts and family trees   137

Notes   155

Bibliography   165

The Colourful Personal Life of Queen Victoria   168

1.

INTRODUCTION

On the evening of Friday 4 September 1846, the royal yacht *Victoria and Albert* steamed into the harbour at Falmouth in Cornwall flying the royal standard. I can see the spot where she moored from my home in St Just-in-Roseland on the other side of the estuary. On board the *Victoria and Albert* were Queen Victoria, her husband Prince Albert, and their two eldest children – five-year-old Vicky (Victoria, the princess royal) and four-year-old Bertie (Albert Edward, prince of Wales). Behind the *Victoria and Albert* steamed three other ships in the royal squadron – the *Fairy, Black Eagle*, and *Garland*. The guns at Pendennis Castle on the headland roared a welcome and the Falmouth waters were alive with boats packed with cheering spectators to greet the queen and her heir[1]. Victoria recorded in her journal that the evening was quite beautiful and the sea as smooth as glass.

The queen's royal visit was a memorable event for the local people; that of her young son even more momentous in the history of Cornwall. As the eldest son of the sovereign, Bertie had been the duke of Cornwall from the moment of his birth. His visit on the royal tour in 1846 was the first time a duke of Cornwall had visited Cornwall for two hundred years!

Queen Victoria's visit to Falmouth was part of her royal tour to Cornwall and the Channel Isles in late summer 1846. This book is an account of that tour focusing particularly on the time that was spent in Cornwall. Over a period of two separate weeks, with a break at Osborne House on the Isle of Wight in the middle, the queen cruised along the south coast of Cornwall and across the English Channel to the Channel Isles off the coast of France. Sketch map 1 on page 130 gives an indication of the route. The royal tour was enthusiastically reported in the world's first illustrated news magazine. *The Illustrated London News* began publication in May 1842 and (in an era before photography) used artists to supplement the text with sketches and drawings. Illustrations 4 (the royal yacht moored off St Michael's Mount) and 48 (the queen arriving at Place House in Fowey) are from *The Illustrated London News*.

The royal cruise was recorded by Victoria herself in the daily journal she kept meticulously throughout her life. Victoria was a keen observer and, as well as official events, her journal is full of interesting details – the royal family were all seasick; Bertie wore a miniature sailor's uniform made by a member of the crew; and the royal carriage accidentally ran over a special constable. Her acerbic comments about the terrifying narrow Cornish lanes, perpendicular hills, and strange sounding Cornish people may still resonate with visitors today. Cornish as a spoken language had died out before Victoria was born but she wrote during the tour that the Cornish 'are a very talkative race, and speak a sort of English, hardly to be understood.'[2].

Victoria revelled in the atmosphere of life on board ship, enjoying breakfast in the deckhouse, watching the sailors sing and dance, and strolling on the deck in moonlight. She wrote that she had never seen the children (Vicky and Bertie) look '... so well & in such spirits'[3]. The queen's enthusiasm for cruising, as explained in chapter 2, was due to the acquisition of a new royal yacht. Launched in 1843, Her Majesty's Yacht (HMY) *Victoria and Albert* was the first royal yacht to be powered by steam and the first in a series that would end with the *Britannia*, decommissioned in 1997. In order to avoid confusion with the term

'Victoria and Albert' used to describe Queen Victoria and her husband Prince Albert, I have used italics for the name of the royal yacht (*Victoria and Albert*) throughout the book.

Chapter 3 is a day-by-day account of the royal visit to Cornwall drawn from Victoria's journal and other contemporary sources. The queen lived on the royal yacht and made excursions ashore to see the sights, meet the local aristocracy in their great houses, and patronise local industries. Sketch map 2 shows the main places in Cornwall that Victoria saw. Chapters 4 to 7 explore further their history and royal connections and share my own experience of visiting. Among her other excursions, the queen toured the spectacular, scenic island castle of St Michael's Mount near Penzance, where the wife of a royal pretender sought refuge while he bid to overthrow King Henry

1. Queen Victoria in the 1840s.

VII; watched a fishing net being drawn beneath Pendennis Castle at Falmouth, grim last stand of the Cornish royalist army of King Charles I during the English Civil War; and, at Place House in Fowey, met the industrialist who was Cornwall's largest employer and known as *The King of Mid-Cornwall*. Albert's visit to the serpentine rock works at Penzance gave a boost to this Cornish industry that flourished during Victoria's reign.

In summer 1846, Queen Victoria was twenty-seven years old and had been married to Prince Albert for six years. Although still in her twenties, Victoria had been on the throne for nine years; she succeeded her uncle (King William IV) in June 1837 just one month after her eighteenth birthday. A young female sovereign was a fresh start for the British monarchy after the scandals of Victoria's elderly male predecessors (her uncles George IV and William IV) with their debts, debaucheries, and illegitimate children. Victoria's public image in the 1840s, as a young wife and the mother of a growing family, was quite different from the gloomy, black-draped widow of later years that has come down to us in history.

2. Victoria and Albert brought a fresh new image to the royal family – this picture from 1843 is called 'The Queen and Prince Albert at home'.

The 1840s were a time of great economic hardship and political unrest – they have been called *the Hungry Forties*. The Irish potato crop failed in 1845 heralding a humanitarian disaster of enormous scale.

Queen Victoria and her family in 1846

The royal party for the visit to Cornwall included Queen Victoria (1819-1901), her husband Prince Albert (1819-1861) and their two eldest children – five-year-old Vicky (Victoria) born in November 1840 (nine months after her parents' wedding); and four-year-old Bertie (Albert Edward) born a year later in November 1841. In six years of married life Victoria had given birth to five babies and three younger children were left behind in the nursery at Osborne House on the Isle of Wight – Alice born in April 1843; Affie (Alfred) in July 1844; and three-month-old Helena born in May 1846. Victoria recorded in her journal that 'Dear little Alice [aged three] had burst into tears, when we drove away' at the start of the tour[4] and how she was delighted on returning home to find that baby Helena was now able to sit up[5].

Victoria's journal of life on board the royal yacht records breakfasting with the children, watching them romp and play, and giving Vicky her lessons. Victoria and Albert were more involved with their children than was usual for aristocratic parents of the time. Family life was very important to Albert, and he enjoyed spending time with his children.

Albert has come down in history as a worthy but rather dull character, so it is endearing to know that he liked to get down on the floor and play games with his children (see illustration 2). Albert was determined to change the image of the British royal family and to bury the shadow of the scandalous Hanoverians in the queen's ancestry. Under Victoria and Albert, the royal family became free from scandal and projected the image of a happy family life.

Victoria was less enthusiastic about being the mother of a large family. She was not naturally maternal and referred to pregnancy and childbirth as 'the shadow side' of marriage[6]. For Victoria, Albert always took first place and perhaps she felt some resentment about his time and attention their children took away from her. Her happiness in family life was based on Albert's delight in being a father. After his early death (Albert died in 1861 aged forty-two) Victoria became a stern and distant figure and her children were always in awe of her, even when grown up.

The crown was not above criticism. There was tremendous disquiet when Victoria chose to take a lavish trip abroad in August 1845, to Albert's old home in Germany, while many of her subjects at home were near starving[7]. If Queen Victoria had to have a holiday, her critics argued in 1845, why could she not take it at home and spend the money in Britain? Such unwelcome and negative publicity could be one reason why Victoria and Albert chose to go to Cornwall (and not abroad) the following year.

Following in Queen Victoria's footsteps to write this book led me to some familiar, much-loved places. Romantic Restormel Castle near Lostwithiel is my favourite historic site to visit in Cornwall. The first duke of Cornwall held his court at Restormel in the fourteenth century and it is still owned by the present duke of Cornwall (Prince Charles). To my surprise, researching Victoria's royal visit also took me to parts of Cornwall I had not been before. My visit to Mount Edgcumbe, home of Victoria's courtiers the earls of Mount Edgcumbe, I am sure will be the first of many. Mount Edgcumbe is in the far south-east of Cornwall just across the water from Plymouth in Devon in an area that is sometimes called 'the forgotten corner of Cornwall'. Another discovery, hidden in trees on the hillside behind Restormel Castle, were the remains of the Restormel Royal Iron Mine that Victoria and Albert went down to see the workings. The mine closed many years ago but toiling up the hill to find the site, as Victoria had done before me, was a special moment.

3. The two symbols frequently found in Cornwall are the 'national flag' called St Piran's Cross and the heraldic badge of the duchy of Cornwall.

Cornwall lies in the far south-west of the UK surrounded by the sea on three sides and cut off from the rest of the country by the river Tamar on the fourth (see map 2). Until relatively recent times Cornwall (Kernow in the Cornish language) was effectively a separate country with its own language, culture, and laws. (Called *stannary law* this governed Cornwall's important tin mining industry.) In 1506, during the reign of King Henry VII, a Venetian ambassador was on board a ship forced to shelter in Falmouth harbour. He wrote

> We are in a very wild place which no human being ever visits ... in the midst of a most barbarous race, so different in language and custom from the Londoners and the rest of England that they are as unintelligible to these last as to the Venetians.[8]

When Victoria travelled to Cornwall in 1846 the only sensible way to get there was still by boat. The famous railway bridge built by Isambard Kingdom Brunel over the Tamar to connect Cornwall with the rest of the country was not in operation until 1859. It was opened by Prince Albert and named the Royal Albert Railway Bridge in his honour. Even today Cornwall is a long way from central government in London. The journey from London to Truro (the capital of Cornwall) takes four and a half hours by rail and longer by road. Cornwall retains a strong sense of its own local identity. The Cornish flag (a white cross on a black background called St Piran's Cross) can be seen flying more frequently across Cornwall than the flags of the United Kingdom (the Union Jack) or England (the red and white cross of St George). The Cornish flag is named for a fifth-century Irish saint who came to Cornwall and performed miracles. St Piran became the patron saint first of Cornish tin miners and then of Cornwall as a whole. Every year St Piran's Day is celebrated in Cornwall on 5 March.

The second symbol frequently encountered in Cornwall is the heraldic badge of the royal duchy of Cornwall (fifteen gold circles representing coins on a black shield[9]). The history of the county of

Cornwall is intertwined with that of the duchy of Cornwall, but the two are not the same. Cornwall is an English county and an area of local government in the same way as, for example, Devon or Wiltshire. The duchy of Cornwall is a private estate first created in 1337 and held since then by the eldest son of the sovereign as duke of Cornwall. While the duchy of Cornwall has substantial landholdings in Cornwall, it does not own the whole county. It also has extensive valuable properties elsewhere such as the Oval Cricket Ground in London, the village of Poundbury in Dorset, and much of Dartmoor in Devon. Chapter 9 is a brief history of the duchy of Cornwall and its royal dukes; chart 4 lists the twenty-four dukes of Cornwall to the present day.

When I moved home to Cornwall, I hoped to combine my love of the area with my fascination for royal history and write a book about the royal dukes of Cornwall in Cornwall. I was shocked to discover that of the twenty dukes who preceded Victoria's son Bertie, only two are known to have visited Cornwall. Cornish money financed the lavish lifestyles of these royal dukes and paid for their wars, but they did not care to go there. My original ideas had to be reworked and over time evolved into this book. All the dukes of Cornwall since Bertie have visited Cornwall.

The royal tour of 1846 began and ended at Osborne House on the Isle of Wight, the summer retreat and holiday home purchased by Victoria and Albert the year before. Just days after their Cornish visit the royal family moved into the new house at Osborne designed and built by Albert. This would become Queen Victoria's favourite home and was where she died on 22 January 1901. Chapter 8 looks at the building of Osborne House and the happy time Victoria and her young family spent there.

I feel privileged to live and write in Cornwall. With a long and spectacular coastline and stunning inland scenery, in my opinion there is no more beautiful place in the world. I hope this book will enable you also to experience Cornwall as Queen Victoria saw it on the royal tour in 1846.

Cornish tin mining and the stannaries

Tin mining in Cornwall is an ancient industry that goes back thousands of years to before the life of Christ. There is a legend attaching to my local church at St Just in Roseland that Jesus came there as a child with Joseph of Arimathea who was a tin trader around the Mediterranean. The areas of Cornwall where tin was mined were called the stannaries. This name derived from the Latin word for tin (stannum). There were four stannaries in Cornwall with their stannary towns at Launceston, Lostwithiel, Truro, and Helston. Cornwall was a major world producer of smelted tin, and the industry was of vital importance to the Cornish economy.

In 1201 King John codified the ancient rights of Cornish tin miners in the first Stannary Charter. Tin miners were exempted from normal laws and taxes and governed instead by stannary law. The stannaries had their own parliament to make the law, law courts to enforce it, and a gaol to punish offenders. Stannary law applied not just to tin mining activities but to all aspects of the lives of those in the tin industry. In return for this special regime all tin production was subject to 'coinage' – a levy or tax on tin. Before sale, ingots of smelted tin had to go to a Coinage Hall to be weighed, assayed (quality checked), and the coinage paid. The term 'coinage' does not come from a coin (money) but from the French word for corner 'le coin'. This is because a corner of each ingot was cut off to assay the metal.

From 1337, when the duchy of Cornwall was created, the stannaries came under the control of the eldest son of the sovereign as duke of Cornwall. The duke was given quasi-royal rights in Cornwall including to appoint the chief official of the stannaries, called the Lord Warden, and to receive the coinage monies. This levy on Cornish tin mining provided a major source of revenue for the heir to the throne for the next five centuries. The coinage levy came to an end only in 1838 and after the Stannary Act of 1896 a separate legal system for tin mining ceased to exist.

By the late nineteenth century tin mining was in decline and many Cornish miners were forced to emigrate to South Africa, Australia, and North America. The last mine called South Crofty near Camborne closed in 1998.

The contents of this book are a blend of historical information and my own impressions from visiting the sights in Cornwall that Victoria saw. The sources consulted are shown in the Notes section and the Bibliography at the back of the book. The appendices have sketch maps, charts and family trees, to supplement the text and the book is illustrated throughout with a mixture of present-day photographs, old prints and postcards, and portraits of Queen Victoria and her family. *Queen Victoria in Cornwall* is not a detailed history of Cornwall or a travel guide. Readers should consult websites or other information for opening hours, ticket prices, and directions.

2.

THE ROYAL YACHT VICTORIA AND ALBERT

Her Majesty's Yacht (HMY) *Victoria and Albert* was launched from Pembroke Dock in Wales (a naval dockyard) on 26 April 1843. She was the first royal yacht to be powered by steam. When Victoria came to the throne in 1837 the royal yacht was a three-masted sailing ship called the *Royal George*, launched in 1817. Victoria had travelled to Edinburgh on the *Royal George* when she visited Scotland for the first time in August 1842. The slow journey up the east coast of England, from Woolwich to the Firth of Forth, took three days in heavy seas and Victoria was seasick. To her great annoyance, the *Royal George* was frequently overtaken by newer and faster steam ships[1]. Victoria determined never to travel under sail again. A steamship was engaged to take the queen back to Woolwich at the end of the visit and she commissioned a new steam yacht.

The *Victoria and Albert* was a twin paddle steamer with a single funnel and a paddle wheel on each side of the ship powered by four hundred and twenty horsepower engines producing a speed of eleven and a half knots[2]. She measured two hundred feet in length and carried two supplementary masts to hoist sails when needed. A smaller steam yacht called the *Fairy* that could operate in shallower waters was commissioned in 1845 as a tender (or support vessel) to the royal yacht. The *Victoria and Albert* also carried a royal barge to be lowered over the side to ferry the royal party between the two vessels and to and from the shore.

4. Her Majesty's Yacht *Victoria and Albert* (on the right) moored off St Michael's Mount during the royal visit to Cornwall in August 1846.

Victoria described her new stream yacht as 'a beautiful vessel with splendid accommodation'[3]. The on-board accommodation included a large salon for receptions and a spacious suite for Victoria and Albert. Victoria wrote that 'Nothing can be nicer or more roomy ...' and 'We feel just as if we were at home, in our charming cabins'[4]. On deck was a round-shaped deck house (or pavilion) with glass windows where Victoria enjoyed taking breakfast and spending time when the royal yacht was at sea. Not all the royal party were so content with their cabins. Charlotte Canning, who accompanied Victoria as lady-in-waiting on the *Victoria and Albert's* maiden voyage, wrote that the queen's cabins were 'delightfully cool and sweet' while those for the household were unbearably hot and stank of 'oil and bilge'[5].

(Bilge water is the foul water that collects at the bottom of the hold). The diarist Charles Greville was shown round the yacht by its captain when the *Victoria and Albert* was launched in 1843. He recorded that

> It is luxuriously fitted up, but everything is sacrificed to the comfort of the Court, the whole ship's company being crammed into wretched dog-holes, officers included. ... They are packed two officers in one berth about seven feet by nine at the most, ...[6]

Greville was clerk to the Privy Council and a court insider during the reigns of George IV, William IV, and Queen Victoria. The publication of his gossipy (and sometimes indiscreet) diaries after his death caused something of a sensation!

The queen and Prince Albert embarked for their maiden voyage on the *Victoria and Albert* from Southampton pier on 28 August 1843. It was raining and the landing stage was wet and slippery. In a gallant gesture reminiscent of Sir Walter Raleigh and Queen Elizabeth I, the mayor and aldermen of Southampton stripped off their scarlet robes and threw these on the ground for Victoria to walk over.

> Her Majesty appeared much gratified by this spontaneous act of attention, and was pleased to step so as to avoid the velvet collars of the robes of office.[7]

During her maiden voyage the *Victoria and Albert* called in at the Isle of Wight (where Victoria and Albert would soon purchase the Osborne Estate) and cruised west along the south coast of England before crossing the Channel to France. There was an incident at Falmouth in Cornwall when the mayors of three local towns (Falmouth, Penryn, and Truro) came out to the *Victoria and Albert* to present addresses of welcome to the queen. In the excitement the mayor of Truro misjudged his leap onto the royal yacht and fell into the sea, robes, and all. He was fished out soaking wet and missed the presentation altogether[8]!

How Victoria succeeded to the throne

Queen Victoria was the only child of Edward Duke of Kent (1767-1820), the fourth son of George III, and Princess Victoire of Saxe-Coburg-Saalfeld (1786-1861). At the time of their marriage in May 1818 the duke was a fifty-year-old bachelor who had recently set aside his mistress of twenty-eight years standing; his new duchess a thirty-one-year-old widow with two children from her first marriage.

Edward's decision to make a late marriage was driven by the death in childbirth in November 1817 of his niece Princess Charlotte of Wales. She died giving birth to a stillborn son. Charlotte was the only child of Edward's eldest brother George, the prince regent (later George IV), and her death meant there was no heir to the British throne in the next generation. Although Edward was only a fourth son, he realised there was now a good chance that his child, if he had one, could succeed to the throne. He also hoped that Parliament might pay off his large debts if he married and fathered the heir. His eldest brother George (first in line to the throne) was estranged from his wife and was unlikely to have more children; the next brother Frederick (second in line) was married but childless; and the third brother William (third in line) had many illegitimate children but was unmarried. After William, Edward was next in the line of succession. His choice of bride was suggested by Charlotte's widower, Prince Leopold, who was the brother of Victoire and eminence gris of the Saxe-Coburg family.

Chart 2 shows how Edward and Victoire's daughter Victoria, born on 24 May 1819 at Kensington Palace in London, succeeded to the British throne in June 1837 at the age of eighteen. Victoria's grandfather George III died in 1820 and was succeeded by Edward's eldest brother as George IV. When George IV died ten years later, he was followed by the third brother as William IV. The second brother (Frederick) was already dead. William IV reigned from 1830 to 1837 and was succeeded by his niece (the daughter of his next younger brother Edward) as Queen Victoria. Edward had died long before, when his daughter was a baby, just days before his father George III in 1820.

The highlight of the maiden voyage was the queen's state visit to King Louis-Philippe of France (1773-1850) at Chateau D'Eu, his summer residence in Normandy. This state visit was Victoria's first trip abroad. It was also the first time the monarchs of the two countries had met since Henry VIII and Francis I were together at *The Field of the Cloth of Gold* in 1520. A flotilla of naval vessels accompanied the *Victoria and Albert* as she steamed the Channel to Le Tréport where Queen Victoria and Prince Albert were met by King Louis-Philippe and his wife, Queen Marie Amelie. The two families were friendly. Louis-Philippe was an old friend of Victoria's father the duke of Kent (from the king's years of exile from France as a young man) and his son was married to Victoria and Albert's

5. Bertie, the young duke of Cornwall, with sailors from the royal yacht.

cousin[9]. After he lost his throne in 1848 Louis-Philippe spent the last years of his life in exile in England.

HMY *Victoria and Albert* was owned and operated by the Royal Navy and manned by a naval crew. Her captain, Lord Adolphus Fitzclarence (1802-1856), was another cousin of the queen but not one that was so readily acknowledged. Adolphus was the seventh of ten illegitimate children of Victoria's uncle, William Duke of Clarence (her father's brother), by his long-term mistress, the actress Mrs Dorothea Jordan. The addition of 'Fitz' to his father's name of Clarence indicated illegitimacy. Victoria's mother, the widowed duchess of Kent, was concerned to protect her young daughter from what she regarded as the shameful taint of illegitimacy of her Fitzclarence cousins. When William became king in 1830 (King William IV), the duchess kept Victoria away from his court and went so far as to leave any room herself if a Fitzclarence entered it[10]. As a result, there was no love lost between William IV and his sister-in-law. When she became queen, Victoria proved more tolerant and kinder to her Fitzclarence cousins than her mother.

6. *The Sailor King* – William IV while duke of Clarence in uniform as an admiral. His illegitimate son Lord Adolphus Fitzclarence was captain of the royal yacht.

William IV (1765-1837) is nicknamed *the Sailor King* because of his service in the Royal Navy as a young man. Adolphus (known as Lolly in the family) followed his father into the navy and went to sea in 1813 aged eleven. The five Fitzclarence daughters were absorbed into the British aristocracy through marriage, but their five brothers were in a more anomalous social position. They badgered their father for titles and increases in their allowances. It is interesting to speculate what might have happened if William IV had married Mrs Jordan. There was no established concept of morganatic marriage in Great Britain (marriage to a commoner where the wife and any children do not take the husband's rank). It is at least possible that Adolphus would have been a royal prince and his eldest brother, George Earl of Munster (1794-1842), become king on their father's death. (Instead, Earl George became a disappointed man who committed suicide by shooting).

When his father succeeded to the British throne as King William IV in 1830, Adolphus was granted the title and precedence of the younger son of a marquess and given command of the royal yacht (at that time the *Royal George*). He did not necessarily expect to keep such preferments in the next reign. Victoria told her first prime minister (Lord Melbourne) how Lord Adolphus had burst into tears when told she would continue to pay their allowances from the late king to him and his siblings. He said this 'was unexpected, for they did not dare to hope for anything.'[11]. Lord Adolphus retained his position as captain of the royal yacht and held it until promoted from captain to admiral in 1853. There are many references to her cousin in Victoria's journal of life on board the *Victoria and Albert*.

With the acquisition of her own steam yacht Victoria took to the life of cruising – '... the semi sailor-gipsy life we lead, is very delightful and must be very healthy.'[12]. She still suffered from seasickness when the sea was choppy but was relieved to note that 'after the first day [at sea] one does get accustomed to the motion'[13]. An aspect of naval life that provided much amusement was the recreations of the sailors. Victoria's journal is peppered with references to the crew singing and dancing to entertain the royal family. She described one dance 'that most curious 'Fisherman's Dance' which they do most amusingly, on their knees, heads, & backs, pulling one another by their legs, ears, noses, & hair, - which highly delighted the children.'[14].

Whenever the *Victoria and Albert* came into harbour, the royal yacht was mobbed by hordes of small boats packed with spectators pushing and jostling to catch a glimpse of the royal family. Victoria was sometimes worried there could be an accident. On the first day of the maiden voyage there was an alarming incident when one of the crew fell into the sea while shoving off the royal barge and disappeared under the water. Fortunately, he could swim and was heaved back into the barge by Lord Adolphus Fitzclarence.

The *Victoria and Albert* was in service as the royal yacht until 1855 when she was replaced by the larger and faster *Victoria and Albert II*. Renamed the *Osborne*, Victoria's first steam yacht continued to ferry the royal family to and from Osborne House on the Isle of Wight before being scrapped in 1868. The *Victoria and Albert II* remained the royal yacht until the end of Victoria's reign. By then the ship was aging and had been put in the shade by the bigger and flashier yachts of the emperor of Germany (Victoria's grandson) called the *Hohenzollern* and the tsar of Russia (married to her granddaughter) called the *Standart*. But Victoria was not happy with the proposals for a replacement and the next yacht called *Victoria and Albert III* was commissioned only at the start of the new reign of Victoria's son, King Edward VII, in 1901.

The last royal yacht was the best known of them all. HMY *Britannia* was launched by Queen Elizabeth II on 16 April 1953 and decommissioned on 11 December 1997. Since then, she has been berthed in Edinburgh and is a popular visitor attraction. In May 2021 British Prime Minister Boris Johnson announced plans for her successor – a new national flagship to promote British interests around the world. It is hoped that following competitive bids construction work could begin in 2022 to have the new ship in the water within three or four years.

3.

THE ROYAL VISIT
DAY BY DAY

Queen Victoria and the royal party embarked from the private pier at Osborne House on the Isle of Wight on the morning of Tuesday 18 August 1846 and returned there at the end of the royal visit to Cornwall on the morning of Wednesday 9 September. The visit was carried out in two parts – from 18 to 24 August when the royal party cruised westwards along the south coast of England so far as Saltash in Cornwall and then crossed the English Channel to visit Guernsey in the Channel Islands; and from 2 to 9 September when the tour restarted in Jersey before moving on to Falmouth and the south coast of Cornwall. Map 1 roughly plots the route of the royal yacht. The days in between the two parts of the visit (25 August to 1 September) were spent back at Osborne House for the queen to attend a meeting there of the Privy Council and to celebrate Albert's twenty-seventh birthday.

This chapter describes the day-by-day itinerary and events for the two weeks of the royal visit based primarily on the coverage in *The Illustrated London News* and the daily entries made by Victoria in her journal. The history and royal connections of the main sights in Cornwall that Victoria visited are further explored in Chapters 4 to 7.

The royal visit in brief

Tuesday 18 August	depart Osborne House on the Isle of Wight; overnight in the Portland Roads off Weymouth in Dorset.
Wednesday 19 August	visit to Abbotsbury Castle.
Thursday 20 August	depart Weymouth; overnight off Dartmouth in Devon.
Friday 21 August	depart Dartmouth; arrive Mount Edgcumbe in Cornwall; visit to Cotehele House.
Saturday 22 August	visit to Mount Edgcumbe House.
Sunday 23 August	depart Mount Edgcumbe; arrive St Peter Port, Guernsey in the Channel Islands.
Monday 24 August	visit to St Peter Port; depart Guernsey for Osborne House on the Isle of Wight.
Tuesday 25 August to Tuesday 1 September	at Osborne House.
Wednesday 2 September	depart Osborne House, Isle of Wight; arrive St Helier, Jersey in the Channel Islands.
Thursday 3 September	visit to St Helier.
Friday 4 September	depart Jersey; overnight at Falmouth in Cornwall.
Saturday 5 September	depart Falmouth; cruise to Land's End; overnight off Marazion in Mount's Bay in Cornwall.
Sunday 6 September	visit to St Michael's Mount; depart Mount's Bay; visit Kynance Cove; arrive Falmouth.
Monday 7 September	cruise up the river Fal.
Tuesday 8 September	depart Falmouth; arrive Fowey in Cornwall; visit to Restormel Castle and iron mine; visit to Place House in Fowey; depart Fowey for the Isle of Wight.
Wednesday 9 September	arrive Osborne House, Isle of Wight.

The party for the royal visit included Queen Victoria, her husband Prince Albert, their two young children, and an entourage of courtiers, attendants, and servants. Victoria was accustomed to living at the centre of a large royal household devoted to looking after her. In her daily journal for the royal visit, she mentions the members of her accompanying suite – ladies in waiting, gentlemen in waiting, naval officers from the royal yacht, governesses for the children (French and German), Albert's secretary, the royal doctor, the Foreign Secretary (the government minister in attendance), and the royal couple's personal adviser Baron Stockmar[1]. Victoria never mentions servants, but they would have been there – dressers, nursery maids, footmen, and more.

The royal family and part of their entourage were accommodated on the royal yacht *Victoria and Albert* with the overflow on another ship called the *Back Eagle*. The royal flotilla that set off also included the *Fairy*, tender (support ship) to the royal yacht. On the fourth day, in Plymouth Sound, they were joined by a fourth ship called the *Garland*.

On the first day at sea, **Tuesday 18 August**, the weather became rough as the royal flotilla left Osborne and the Isle of Wight behind. Lord Adolphus Fitzclarence, captain of the royal yacht *Victoria and Albert*, told the queen he had rarely experienced a worse sea. Victoria, her husband, and the children were all seasick. Albert had a history as a poor sailor and had famously arrived in England for his wedding looking 'the colour of a wax candle' after a dreadful Channel crossing[2]. Victoria wrote in her journal for that first day at sea how it was a merciful relief when they anchored for the night in the Portland Roads near Weymouth on the coast of Dorset and how she longed to be back on dry land at Osborne again!

The weather was still bad on **Wednesday 19 August** but despite the rain the royal party came ashore at Weymouth in the afternoon and drove a few miles inland to see the gardens at Abbotsbury Castle. Unfortunately, the owner (the Whig politician Lord Ilchester) was not at home. Weymouth was the favoured seaside resort of Victoria's grandparents, King George III and Queen Charlotte, but Victoria was not impressed on this visit, describing it as an unattractive place and the people of the villages they drove through as looking poor and dirty. Perhaps the weather had made her grumpy.

7. Mount Edgcumbe House on Plymouth Sound, home of the earls of Mount Edgcumbe.

The queen's mood lifted on the morning of **Thursday 20 August,** and she enjoyed the scenery as the *Victoria and Albert* steamed westward along the coast of Devon. The royal yacht dropped anchor off Lyme Regis for breakfast and in Babbacombe Bay (off Torquay) for lunch. Victoria enthused about the red cliffs of Babbacombe and thought she could easily imagine nymphs appearing on them. (Nymphs are mythical spirits in the form of beautiful young women.) But the weather worsened in the afternoon and the plan to reach Plymouth that day had to be abandoned. With a stormy sea and in such pouring rain that the decks were swimming with water the royal yacht put into Dartmouth for the night.

Friday 21 August dawned a fine morning and the royal flotilla got under way early. By breakfast time they arrived in Plymouth Sound in south-east Cornwall. They came to anchor in Barn Pool, a small bay below Mount Edgcumbe House, home of the earls of Mount Edgcumbe. A vibrant watercolour in the Royal Collection by local Cornish artist Nicholas Condy (1793-1857) shows the royal yacht *Victoria and Albert* steaming into Barn Pool accompanied by the *Fairy* and *Black Eagle*[3]. Photography was still in its infancy (Victoria had her photograph taken for the first time in 1844 or 1845) and the royal couple commissioned drawings and watercolours to record their travels. Arranging these in albums was a favourite way for them to spend an evening.

In the early afternoon Victoria and Albert transferred from the *Victoria and Albert* to the smaller *Fairy* for a river cruise (see map 3). They went partway up the Lynher River (in her journal Victoria calls it by an alternative name of St Germans River) to stop beneath Trematon Castle for lunch. This ancient castle, built to guard the southern entry to Cornwall by Robert Count of Mortain, the half-brother of William *the Conqueror*, was one of the properties granted to the duchy of Cornwall on its formation in 1337. Victoria noted in her journal that it still belonged to her young son Bertie as the duke of Cornwall.

After lunch the *Fairy* cruised up the Tamar River so far as Cotehele Quay. The Tamar forms the boundary between the counties of Cornwall and Devon and is a natural landmark that divides Cornwall from the rest of the UK (map 2). Victoria enthused that as they went up the Tamar 'the scenery becomes quite beautiful – richly wooded hills, and the trees growing down to the water's edge – the river winding so much (like the Rhine)'[4]. She thought the finest feature of the river was Pentillie Castle situated where the Tamar makes a deep u-bend above Saltash. Pentillie (illustration 8) was built by a colourful character called Sir James Tillie in the early eighteenth century. Still owned within his extended family it is now a glamorous wedding and event venue.

At Cotehele Quay, Victoria and Albert came ashore and drove up the steep hill to see 'the very curious old house of Cotehele' preserved 'as it was in the time of Henry VII'. Cotehele was the ancestral home of the earls of Mount Edgcumbe. Rebuilt by Sir Richard Edgcumbe,

8. Pentillie Castle on the river Tamar near Saltash.

who was a leading courtier to King Henry VII, the house is changed little today since Tudor times. Another watercolour by Nicholas Condy in the Royal Collection shows Victoria and Albert being rowed ashore from the *Fairy* in the royal barge to Cotehele Quay[5]. Condy was born on the Tamar and initially followed a military career, turning to painting after the Napoleonic Wars (ended 1815). His beautiful watercolours illustrated the first guidebook to Cotehele, published in 1840[6]. He also painted a gorgeous series of views of Mount Edgcumbe in 1849[7]. The history and royal connections of both Edgcumbe great houses, Cotehele and Mount Edgcumbe, are explored further in chapter 4.

Albert left the royal yacht early in the morning on **Saturday 22 August** to visit Dartmoor in Devon. (A large part of Dartmoor was owned by his son Bertie as the duke of Cornwall.) Victoria breakfasted on board the royal yacht with Vicky and Bertie and then took them ashore to visit Mount Edgcumbe. The royal party were greeted by crowds of spectators when they landed on the beach at Barn Pool to be received by Earl Ernest Augustus of Mount Edgcumbe and his wife

Countess Caroline. They drove to Mount Edgcumbe House on what Victoria described as 'a lovely drive along the road overhanging the bay, commanding most beautiful views on all sides'[8]. After lunch Victoria sat in the Gallery in the West Wing at Mount Edgcumbe and sketched the view of the sea. Later in the afternoon, after Albert's return from Dartmoor, the royal couple went aboard the *Fairy* to cruise around Plymouth Sound and be rowed by barge up the river Plym (another river that meets the sea in Plymouth Sound) to see the exterior of Saltram House in Devon owned by the earl of Morley.

The intention had been to return to Osborne House on **Sunday 23 August** for Victoria to attend a meeting there of the Privy Council. But the date of the council was put back, so the decision was taken after discussion with Lord Adolphus Fitzclarence to make a surprise visit to Guernsey in the Channel Islands instead. The weather continued fine, and the sea was as smooth as oil, as the royal flotilla steamed across the English Channel to arrive at St Pierre (St Peter Port), the capital of Guernsey, in the early evening. When the royal party came on deck after dinner, Victoria was delighted to see the town illuminated, despite the short notice of her visit. The Channel Islands are *crown dependencies* (self-governing possessions of the British Crown), and Victoria proudly noted that she was the first British sovereign to visit the islands since King John (1166-1216).

Flags were flying, crowds cheering, and a choir of ladies in white dresses sang the national anthem, when Victoria landed on the pier in St Peter Port on the morning of **Monday 24 August**. With Albert she drove in an open carriage through streets lined with the local militia (local reserve troops) to Fort George, the island's military headquarters. Here the lieutenant governor (representative of the British monarch in Guernsey) presented the queen with the keys of the town. Unfortunately, the streets were narrow and, in the melee as they approached the Fort, the royal carriage accidentally ran over a special constable. 'Mercifully, when picked up it was found no bones were broken, & that he was only very faint.'[9].

Queen Victoria's Journal

Queen Victoria was a prodigious diarist and kept a journal (or diary) from the age of thirteen. For nearly seventy years she diligently recorded the daily events of her life. The first entry was made on 1 August 1832 in a book given to Victoria by her mother to record their visit to Wales. The last (brief) entry was dictated on 13 January 1901 only nine days before Victoria died. Failing health and poor eyesight meant the queen was no longer able to write the journal herself.

Unfortunately, Victoria's journal was censored after her death by her youngest daughter Beatrice. Victoria entrusted the journal to Beatrice with instructions to edit it for posterity. It was a Herculean task that took nearly forty years. Beatrice wrote out her mother's entries, amending or omitting anything she considered sensitive, and destroyed the original volumes as she went. When she had finished there were one hundred and eleven volumes in Beatrice's handwriting. Only thirteen original volumes in Victoria's handwriting survived, covering the period before she came to the throne in June 1837.

Victoria's grandson, King George V, was unhappy about the loss of what he knew were irreplaceable historical documents. However, he felt unable to intervene since his aunt Beatrice was only doing what her mother had instructed.

Surviving fragments of Victoria's original entries give a glimpse of how Beatrice wielded the censor's pen. For example, in August 1845 Victoria and Albert were guests of the king and queen of Prussia at their castle on the Rhine in Germany. Victoria wrote in her journal that their hosts (married over twenty years) were like a young married couple; that she had seen them kiss one another; and how the queen called her husband 'liebchen' (sweetheart). Beatrice's edited version says blandly only that they were a most devoted couple.

Victoria's journal is kept in the Royal Archives at Windsor Castle. By a special initiative of Queen Elizabeth II's diamond jubilee year of 2012 it is available to view online at www.queenvictoriasjournals.org

From Fort George Victoria's carriage returned at a fast pace to the pier. By early afternoon the royal flotilla had weighed anchor and set steam for the Isle of Wight where they arrived back at Osborne on the morning of **Tuesday 25 August**.

Wednesday 26 August was Albert's twenty-seventh birthday. His children presented their father with bouquets of flowers and Victoria's gifts included a valuable Italian Renaissance painting by Pietro Perugino and ornaments for the new house at Osborne that Albert was building and was now near completion (see chapter 8). On **Saturday 29 August** the prince's birthday was celebrated with a rural fete at Osborne for estate workers and the hundreds of building labourers working on the new house. After a lavish meal in a marquee on the lawn there were country dances and rural sports such as cricket, running races, sack races, and leapfrog. Victoria 'never saw so much fun and people more cheery & pleased' proving that 'the English can, & like to enjoy themselves, just as much as any other nationality & are not so

9. Four-year-old Bertie in 1846 wearing a miniature sailor's uniform made by the tailor on the royal yacht.

dull and grave, as some wish to represent them to be.'[10]. Her young children were at the fete having a wonderful time until nearly half past six in the evening.

For the second week of the royal visit to Cornwall the royal party embarked from Osborne Pier early in the morning of **Wednesday 2 September**. The royal flotilla set off for the Channel Islands to arrive in St Aubin's Bay off St Helier, the capital of Jersey, in the evening. Albert compared the brilliant blue waters of St Aubin's Bay to the Bay of Naples in Italy. During the day at sea four-year-old Bertie appeared on deck of the *Victoria and Albert*, to the delight of its cheering crew, wearing a miniature version of a sailor's uniform. Bertie was entered on the books of the royal yacht as a midshipman (apprentice officer) and his sailor suit was made by the ship's tailor who did the uniforms for the crew. It was reported that 'The sailors gave the Royal Sailor nine times nine [extended cheering] and when this was over he ordered grog [diluted rum] to be given to each of them.'[11].

Bertie's sailor suit was immortalised in a portrait of the little boy done the same year by the royal portrait painter Franz Xaver Winterhalter (see illustration 9). It set the fashion as a must-have item of clothing for boy princes right up to World War I. Queen Elizabeth II's father, King George VI born in 1895, was often photographed as a child wearing a sailor suit.

The crowds were immense when the queen landed at Victoria Harbour in St Helier on the morning of **Thursday 3 September**. Jersey had been given more notice of the royal visit than its neighbour (Guernsey) and St Helier was beautifully decorated with arches of flowers and greenery. Victoria's path was strewn with flowers as she walked along the pier to a dais under a canopy where she received an address of welcome from the States (parliament) of Jersey. The States walked in front of the royal carriage in a slow procession through the town to Government House. Victoria noticed everyone was speaking French and that one stand for spectators was filled with Frenchwomen from Granville in Normandy (just a few miles across the sea) wearing their local costume.

The lieutenant governor of Jersey was elderly and unwell, and the queen did not alight from her carriage at Government House. From here the royal carriage speeded up for a lightening tour of the interior of the island before returning to the royal yacht. Victoria drove past the ancient tower of La Hougue Bie and visited thirteenth-century

Gorey castle (Mont Orgueil) built by King John as a defence against the French. The crowds were even greater when they got back to St Helier pier and Victoria complained that the militia who should have been keeping order did more harm than good. The weather was hot and sunny, and the queen was suffering from the heat and glare. She spent the afternoon quietly below decks on the *Victoria and Albert*.

10. St Mawes Castle with Pendennis Castle Falmouth
on the headland in the distance.

Friday 4 September was another beautiful morning and the royal flotilla set off across the English Channel for Falmouth in Cornwall. The sea was choppy, and the *Victoria and Albert* rolled with the swell, so the crew put up sails to steady her. (I am assured by a friend in the Merchant Navy that this technique does work.) Victoria remained on deck for much of the journey walking and talking, with the children running around, and watching the crew play navy games. Their games included *single stick* (a rudimentary form of fencing with wooden cudgels) and *swing* (or *swinging*) *the monkey*. In this game a sailor is suspended upside down off the ground by his ankles and given a stick. If he can strike one of his taunting colleagues, then the two men swap places! These games may sound brutal but perhaps they were a way of keeping the sailors physically fit?

The royal flotilla steamed into Falmouth at seven o'clock that evening surrounded by hordes of boats and with thousands of cheering spectators lining the shore. When the *Victoria and Albert* was sighted from Pendennis Castle half an hour earlier everyone in Falmouth rushed down to the water. The 'twin' castles of Pendennis at Falmouth and St Mawes on the opposite side of the Carrick Roads (the estuary of the river Fal) were built by Henry VIII as part of the defences against foreign invasion along the south coast of England. Their history and royal connections are explored further in chapter 6. The queen and Prince Albert stood on deck as the royal yacht came into port at Falmouth; later in the evening they came out on deck again to see fireworks in honour of their visit and admire the illuminations on land and water. The remaining days of the royal tour would take place in Cornwall with an itinerary arranged by Richard Taylor, mineral agent for the duchy of Cornwall, who joined the royal party at Falmouth.

During the morning of **Saturday 5 September,** the *Victoria and Albert* steamed round the Lizard peninsula (see map 4) and then further west past the Longships lighthouse at Land's End before turning back to anchor in Mount's Bay near Penzance. As the royal flotilla came into the bay, the day suddenly brightened, and the sun brilliantly lit up the story-book castle perched high on the top of St Michael's Mount.

In the afternoon Victoria, Albert and the children boarded the royal barge to transfer from the *Victoria and Albert* to the *Fairy* for a cruise around St Michael's Mount. This is a tidal island connected to the land at low tide but surrounded by the sea at high tide. Clambering into and out of the barge in the sea swell was not an easy manoeuvre, particularly for ladies with their long skirts and cumbersome clothes. The royal barge was rowed through an avenue of boats including what Victoria described as the curious large boats of Cornish pilchard fishermen. (Pilchard fishing was a vital part of the Cornish economy during the nineteenth century.) While Albert went ashore to visit a tin smelting plant and the serpentine rock works at Penzance, Victoria and the children returned to the royal yacht. The shoals of boats crowding around the *Victoria and Albert* were filled with sightseers hoping to catch a glimpse of the queen and shouting 'Three cheers for the duke of Cornwall' whenever Bertie appeared on deck. While the royal yacht was moored in Mount's Bay Victoria began a watercolour painting (still in the Royal Collection) of St Michaels' Mount[12].

On the morning of **Sunday 6 September** Victoria and Albert landed at the small harbour of St Michael's Mount and climbed up a rugged winding path over rocks to visit the castle on the peak. St Michael's Mount was the home of the St Aubyn family but due to a difficulty over the inheritance (see chapter 5) there was no St Aubyn in residence to greet the queen. Victoria and Albert were shown round the castle by the housekeeper, whom the queen described as '... a nice, tidy old woman ...'[13]. Victoria's journal records curiosities of St Michael's Mount that still intrigue visitors today, including St Michael's Chair. This is a rough stone seat fixed to the battlements at the top of the church tower that hangs over a precipice around one hundred feet deep[14].

11. The castle on St Michael's Mount, home of the St Aubyn family.

The housekeeper relayed the legend that whichever of an engaged couple sits in this terrifying perch first will have the whip hand in the relationship! Albert went up to look and thought it the most awkward place to climb into. The housekeeper assured them, that nevertheless, many couples tried it. The prince also played the church organ and descended to a small underground chamber beneath the church (Victoria called it the dungeon) where the skeleton of a very tall man had been discovered! To this day it is not known who he was or how he came to be interred[15]. For more on the history of St Michael's Mount and its connection with an attempt to overthrow the throne in Tudor times see chapter 5.

After their return to the *Victoria and Albert* a Sunday morning church service was held on deck. Bertie appeared on muster with his sailor suit newly laundered thanks to improvisation by one of the ship's crew. Like any normal four-year-old the little duke of Cornwall had got his clothes grubby. The sailor washed and dried the suit overnight and, with no mangle or iron available, sat on it to get out the creases. Lord Adolphus Fitzclarence, captain of the royal yacht, commented on Bertie's smart appearance and explained the circumstances to his amused parents[16].

In the afternoon the royal flotilla got underway to return to Falmouth. During the journey they stopped at Kynance Cove on the Lizard peninsula where Albert went ashore to look at the rock formations. The local rock, called serpentine, is unique to this part of Cornwall. Albert picked up many fine specimens of the rock marked with red and green veins. The prince's enthusiasm for serpentine as an ornamental stone would boost the development of this Victorian Cornish industry. There is more about Kynance Cove and the story of the serpentine industry in chapter 5.

From early in the morning of **Monday 7 September** the *Victoria and Albert* was surrounded at Falmouth by boats of cheering and noisy sightseers. It was estimated that at least ten thousand people were packed into the town[17]. During the morning the town councillors from Penryn (a port five miles upstream from Falmouth) came aboard the royal yacht to present a loyal address to the queen and meet the duke of Cornwall. When Albert returned in the afternoon from visiting local mines and the town of Truro, the royal family boarded the *Fairy* to explore the Carrick Roads and the river Fal. For the route of their cruise, see map 5. Victoria enjoyed the beauty of the river with its gentle creeks and thought the prettiest part was around the King Harry Ferry. This ancient ferry takes its name from King Henry VI (not as often thought from Henry VIII) to whom a nearby chapel was dedicated. The ferry is still in operation today and considered one of the ten most scenic ferry trips in the world[18].

12. Tregothnan on the river Fal above King Harry Ferry, home of Lord Falmouth.

Victoria's journal mentions the great houses on the banks of the Fal as the *Fairy* cruised upriver – Trefusis House at Flushing, home to the Trefusis family since the thirteenth century; Carclew near Mylor Bridge, then home of Sir Charles Lemon but destroyed by a fire in 1934; and the Tregothnan estate of Lord Falmouth, where she admired 'a beautiful little Boat House, quiet in the woods ...'[19]. The *Fairy* steamed up the river Truro to within sight of the town of Truro and to a bend in the river called Sunny Corner where the whole population flocked out of the town, on foot and in carts, to cheer the royal party. This area on the outskirts of Truro is still an important leisure facility with sports ground, municipal park, moorings, fishing, and water sports. A regular foot passenger ferry service operates between Truro and Falmouth, so it is possible to take the same boat trip as enjoyed by Victoria.

13. Sunny Corner at Truro, the far point of Victoria's cruise up the river Fal.

The excitements of the royal day at Falmouth were still not over. After returning downriver the *Fairy* steamed round Pendennis Castle headland to Swanpool (map 5) where Victoria enthused that the sea water was extraordinarily clear and transparent as glass. The royal family had been invited to see a fishing net being drawn off the beach at Swanpool by 'A Quaker gentleman, a Mr Fox, who ... has sent us flowers, fruits & all sorts of things'. This was Alfred Fox, from the influential Quaker Fox family who had many business interests in

Falmouth and the local area. Alfred built Glendurgan House on the Helford River near Falmouth and established its beautiful gardens now owned by the National Trust[20]. The produce he sent to the royal yacht from Glendurgan included a grapefruit, then a great curiosity in Britain[21]. Seine fishing involves casting the net over a wide area and then drawing it in to gather the fish. Mr Fox hoped to show the queen a variety of the local fish but in the event not a single one was caught! In the evening after dinner Victoria and Albert came out on deck to enjoy the effect of two boats with miners carrying torches.

The royal flotilla left Falmouth early on **Tuesday 8 September** for Fowey harbour where Victoria and Albert came ashore to visit Restormel Castle (see map 6). This was owned by Bertie as the duke of Cornwall. Judging by the comments in her journal, Victoria did not much enjoy the approximately ten-mile carriage drive to Restormel near the town of Lostwithiel '... through some of the narrowest streets

14. Restormel Castle as a romantic landscape ruin
(picture from the late eighteenth century).

I ever saw in England ... perpendicular hills, which made our progress really quite alarming ... for a long way on bad narrow roads ...'. She was more impressed by the ruined castle itself 'surrounded by woods ... covered with ivy ...'[22].

Restormel Castle was built by Edmund Earl of Cornwall in the late thirteenth century and granted to the duchy of Cornwall on its creation in 1337. The first duke of Cornwall, Edward of Woodstock known as *the Black Prince*, held his court at Restormel on two occasions. The castle was largely neglected by the later dukes but was enjoying something of a resurgence at the time of Victoria's visit as a romantic ruin and picturesque landscape feature. The tenant of nearby Restormel Manor, also owned by the duchy of Cornwall, had incorporated it into his garden vistas. Chapter 7 has more on the history of Restormel and its strong association with *the Black Prince*.

From Restormel the royal party walked half a mile uphill across duchy of Cornwall land to the Restormel Iron Mine. The mine operators had been notified of the intended visit the evening before and had lined out a mine wagon with straw and green baize to '... make our beloved Queen and her august Consort as comfortable as possible during their subterraneous excursion.'[23]. The mine was entered by a gently sloping tunnel called an adit (rather than a vertical shaft) and the wagon or truck with Victoria and Albert was dragged in by the miners. The tunnel was low and narrow, and Victoria described how there was no space between the truck and the tunnel wall and only just enough headroom. At the mine face the royal couple got out of the wagon and Albert wielded a pick to knock out some iron ore as a souvenir. When writing up her journal for that day Victoria sketched the miners in their 'curious woollen dress' and cap where 'they generally have a candle stuck in front'[24]. The queen was much praised for her 'courage and firmness' during the visit[25] and the mine was renamed the Restormel Royal Iron Mine in her honour.

On the return journey to Fowey the royal carriage halted briefly in Lostwithiel for Victoria to receive a loyal address from the town council.

Lostwithiel was the administrative centre for the duchy of Cornwall and site of the Duchy Palace built by Edmund Earl of Cornwall in the late thirteenth century. The Duchy Palace was the equivalent of Westminster Palace for the stannaries in Cornwall (tin mining areas), complete with its parliament, courts and a gaol, exchequer, and the Coinage Hall (where the tin miners came to have their metal assayed and pay the coinage levy). Only the rump of the buildings remains today – the outside is still impressive, but the inside is a shop.

15. Place House in Fowey was rebuilt by Joseph Thomas Treffry, known as *the King of Mid Cornwall*.

In Fowey, Victoria and Albert were the guests at Place House of Mr Joseph Thomas Treffry sometimes known as *The King of Mid Cornwall*[26]. Treffry was the owner of extensive mine, quarry, and railway interests and said to be the largest employer in the west of England. He inherited Place through his mother and used his vast wealth to remodel the medieval mansion in fashionable mock-gothic style. Victoria commented on the Porphyry Hall built entirely of stone from Treffry's own quarries.

From Place House the royal couple walked back to the harbour through the narrow streets of Fowey 'totally *unguarded*, except by her loyal and faithful Cornishmen'[27]. That afternoon the royal flotilla set off to return to Osborne on the Isle of Wight where they arrived on the morning of **Wednesday 9 September**. Victoria's cruise to Cornwall and the life of independence she enjoyed on board was over. Five days later (on **14 September 1846**) the royal family slept for the first time in the new Osborne House (see chapter 8).

4.

COTEHELE AND MOUNT EDGCUMBE

After a difficult three-day journey from the Isle of Wight in rough seas and poor weather the royal yacht *Victoria and Albert* came to anchor in Plymouth Sound off the south-east coast of Cornwall on the morning of Friday 21 August 1846 (see map 3). In the afternoon Queen Victoria and Prince Albert went on board the *Fairy* (tender to the royal yacht) to enjoy an excursion in better weather and the calmer waters of the river Tamar. They came ashore at Cotehele to visit the ancestral home of the earls of Mount Edgcumbe. The following day (Saturday 22 August) Victoria was a guest at the main family home at Mount Edgcumbe, off which the royal yacht was moored.

Although only a few miles apart, the houses occupy very different positions. Cotehele is hidden away in quiet countryside upriver; Mount Edgcumbe prominent on a headland overlooking the busy waters of Plymouth Sound. The colourful history of these two great houses is intertwined with that of the Edgcumbe family as they rose in rank from gentlemen farmers to peers of the realm. This chapter explores their story and shares my experience of visiting their houses. Chart 5 has a list of the Edgcumbes of Cotehele and Mount Edgcumbe.

16. Earl Kenelm Mount Edgcumbe and Countess Lilian. The earl gave Cotehele to the National Trust and rebuilt Mount Edgcumbe, destroyed in World War II. (The Box, Plymouth/Mount Edgcumbe Collection)

The Edgcumbe great houses are now museums open to the public. Cotehele was transferred to the National Trust by the sixth earl of Mount Edgcumbe in 1947 in lieu of inheritance taxes, and as a memorial to his heir killed in action during World War II. It is one of the National Trust's top attractions in Cornwall and a pleasure to visit. With the prospect of more taxes looming, the seventh earl sold Mount Edgcumbe to Cornwall County Council and Plymouth City Council in 1971. Discovering Mount Edgcumbe was an exciting part of researching this book. Despite living in Cornwall this was the first time I had been there. The area is sometimes called 'the forgotten corner of Cornwall' and chatting to others I found mine was not a unique experience. This hidden treasure is one of Cornwall's glories!

Cotehele (historically sometimes spelt Cothele) came into the possession of the Edgcumbe family in 1353 through the marriage of William Edgcumbe (died 1379/80) to the heiress Hillaria de Cotehele. It would be owned by their descendants for six hundred years. The name (pronounced coat-heel) probably derives from the old Cornish words *cote* (wood) and *hele* (estuary). I visited (like Victoria) with my husband on a day in late summer. An early mist was still hanging in the air and the first fallen leaves drifting across the grass. Cotehele sits behind a tangle of small roads and is not easy to find. We got lost when the car satellite navigation directed us down an impossibly narrow lane with grass growing in the middle! Then suddenly out of the mist Cotehele Quay emerged through the trees. This is where Victoria and Albert landed and drove up the steep drive to 'the very curious old house of Cotehele'[1]. The exterior has changed little since Tudor times when it was rebuilt by William and Hillaria's great-grandson Richard Edgcumbe (1443-1489).

By backing the eventual winner in the Wars of the Roses (1455-1485) Richard Edgcumbe was the founder of the family fortunes. Like many Cornish gentry he supported Henry Tudor's claim to the English throne against King Richard III. The legend goes that Richard Edgcumbe used a clever ruse to evade arrest for treason when Richard III's chief henchman in Cornwall, called Sir Henry Bodrugan, pursued him to Cotehele in 1483. He hid in the trees on the riverbank, weighted his hat with stones, and threw it into the Tamar to feign death by drowning! His great-great-grandson wrote up the story in a famous book published in 1602/1603. Called *The Survey of Cornwall* by Richard Carew it is a fascinating picture of life as it was in Cornwall over four hundred years ago. It has been called the most important book ever written about Cornwall.

... these rangers were fast at his heels, who looking down after the noise and seeing the cap swimming thereon, supposed that he had desperately drowned himself, gave up their further hunting, and left him liberty to shift away and ship over into Brittany ...[2]

Richard Edgcumbe escaped to join Henry Tudor and fight alongside him at the battle of Bosworth Field in 1485 when Richard III was defeated. He was knighted on the battlefield by the new king and rewarded with lands and preferments in Cornwall, including those previously held by his enemy Sir Henry Bodrugan. In a neat twist to the legend, the newly knighted Sir Richard now pursued Bodrugan to his home near Mevagissey in Cornwall where Sir Henry leapt off the cliff and escaped by ship[3]. The place is still known as Bodrugan's Leap.

The new Sir Richard Edgcumbe was a favoured courtier and held high positions at Henry VII's court. He became a privy councillor,

17. Cotehele, ancestral home of the Edgcumbe family, in a picture from the early nineteenth century.

comptroller of the royal household and undertook important diplomatic missions for the king[4]. The Edgcumbe family remained in favour at later Tudor courts. Richard's son Sir Piers (1468-1539) was with Henry VIII at *The Field of the Cloth of Gold* (the diplomatic extravaganza in 1520 when Henry met King Francis I of France in northern France). Sir Piers' great-granddaughter Margaret was maid of honour to Queen Elizabeth I. A portrait of Margaret, as a formidable old lady, hangs in the entrance to Mount Edgcumbe House[5].

Mount Edgcumbe also came into the family through marriage with an heiress. In 1493 Sir Piers married Joan Durnford whose dowry included lands on both banks at the mouth of the river Tamar. The lands on the western side became the Mount Edgcumbe estate; those across the river at Stonehouse (now part of Plymouth) remained in the family ownership until sold in the second half of the eighteenth century when the naval dockyards at Plymouth were expanding. Joan's dowry also included rights to a ferry connecting these lands on either side of the river. Called the Cremyll ferry, this is still running today and a delightful way to arrive at Mount Edgcumbe from Plymouth. Rights to operate the Cremyll ferry remained in Edgcumbe family ownership until the twentieth century.

In 1515 Henry VIII granted Sir Piers Edgcumbe permission to enclose a deer park at Mount Edgcumbe and his son, Sir Richard Edgcumbe II (1497-1562), built Mount Edgcumbe House. (Richard and Piers were popular names in the Edgcumbe family and were used alternatively for sons across the centuries.) Mount Edgcumbe House was built between 1547 and 1550 to a design that was radical for its time. Historically, Tudor mansions such as Cotehele were aligned to face inward with several wings around an internal courtyard or courtyards. The entrance to Cotehele is through an enchanting internal courtyard with Tudor mullion windows and arched doorways (see illustration 18). In contrast, Mount Edgcumbe was built as a single wing with towers on each corner of the building and the rooms arranged around a central hall top-lit by clerestory (roof-level) windows. The house is orientated outwards with spectacular views over the estate to Plymouth Sound and the river Tamar. The finished result was so pleasing that Mount Edgcumbe soon became the main family residence. Cotehele was relegated to secondary status and lived in only occasionally.

As the Edgcumbes rose through the ranks of the nobility, Mount Edgcumbe was extended and enhanced but Cotehele remained largely unchanged. The family became proud of their historic showpiece and enjoyed showing visitors around. King George III and Queen Charlotte toured the house when they visited Cotehele in August 1789. Their granddaughter Victoria was shown the rooms in the same order when she came with Albert fifty-seven years later, on 21 August 1846. Quite extraordinarily, visitors still take the same route through the house today! The first guidebook to Cotehele was published as long ago as 1840. Called *Cothele on the Banks of the Tamar* it has descriptions of each room with beautiful colour illustrations by local Cornish artist Nicholas Condy (1793-1857). Reading the guidebook (courtesy of the National Trust) was one of the joys of my research. Here is the romantic opening paragraph of the text by the Reverend F V J Arundell.

18. The enchanting courtyard at Cotehele
with Tudor mullion windows and arched doorways.

Who has not heard of the surpassing beauties of the River Tamar? To the residents in Cornwall and Devonshire this enchanting river is well known, and by them its beauties are well appreciated; but, for the information of those who live in other parts of England, it may be proper to state, that, in the most picturesque part of this celebrated stream, is an ancient mansion, the property of Earl Mount Edgecumbe, called COTHELE, which, from its situation, embosomed in woods of gigantic chesnuts [chestnuts] and oak, the ancient form of its buildings – so ancient in part, as to be almost clouded in mystery – and its historical associations, throws a fairy-like illusion over the whole river.[6]

Copies of the illustrations from the 1840 guidebook are on display in each room at Cotehele and show how little they have changed in the last two hundred years. Each room also has a booklet packed with interesting information about its history and contents, with colourful anecdotes and family trees. I read everything[7]! The largest and most impressive room is the Tudor Hall on the ground floor where the tour begins. Queen Charlotte described this as

... a large Hall full of Old Armour and Swords and Old Carved Chairs of the Times'[8]

At Christmas, in a tradition going back to the 1950s, the Tudor Hall is decorated with a sixty-foot-long green garland (eighteen metres) made on site with fresh pittosporum (an evergreen shrub) and up to thirty thousand flowers grown and dried at Cotehele. Many visitors come specially to see this.

A bedroom at the top of the north-west tower at Cotehele is named the King Charles's Room in celebration that the king might have slept here during the English Civil War (1642-1651). The 1840 guidebook states this was probably Charles I in September 1644 on a march from

19. Queen Charlotte described the Tudor Hall at Cotehele as 'A large Hall full of Old Armour and Swords and Old Carved Chairs of the Times'.

Liskeard to Exeter; other accounts suggest it was his son, the future Charles II, during his escape to the Scilly Isles in 1646. Both claims are unproven[9]. The room was not given its name until over a century later, so perhaps it was just smart marketing.

Colonel Sir Piers Edgcumbe III (c1610-1666) was a committed royalist (a cavalier) during the Civil War. As Mount Edgcumbe was vulnerable to raids by the equally staunch parliamentarians (roundheads) just across the water in Plymouth, he moved the family to the greater security of their ancestral home at Cotehele. When the royalist army in Cornwall surrendered to Parliament in 1646 Colonel Sir Piers III was fortunate to escape with just a hefty fine and not to forfeit his estates. The loyalty of the Edgcumbes was recognised when the monarchy was restored, and King Charles II visited Mount Edgcumbe[10].

Both Queen Charlotte and her granddaughter Queen Victoria noticed the old tapestries at Cotehele. When Lord Richard Edgcumbe I (1680-1758) was upgraded in rank from knight to baron in 1742 he updated and remodelled Mount Edgcumbe House. The outmoded furniture and fittings were sent up the river to Cotehele and have been there ever since. The walls of the dining room (next door to the Tudor Hall) at Cotehele are hung end to end with tapestries. In a make-do-and-mend approach, these have been cut and patched to fit the space regardless that design and patterns do not match. Lord Richard I was a Whig Politian and a close associate of Prime Minister Robert Walpole. Corruption in politics was rife and as leader of the Whig organisation in Cornwall and the south-west, Lord Richard I probably knew 'where the bodies were buried'. It is alleged that he was raised to the peerage as the first baron Edgcumbe only so that he could not be called to testify against Walpole in the House of Commons[11]!

20. Mount Edgcumbe in 1830.

Lord Richard I was an early patron of the famous portrait painter Sir Joshua Reynolds who was born nearby in Plymouth. Sadly, the Edgcumbe collection of family portraits by Reynolds went up in flames when Mount Edgcumbe House was hit by an incendiary bomb during World War II. The only Reynolds portrait to survive was that of Lord Richard I's eldest son, Lord Richard II (1716-1761).

Ranks of the nobility

Nobility in England is classified in seven ranks or levels. At the bottom of the rankings are **knights** and above them **baronets** both carrying the address of 'Sir' (for example Sir Richard Edgcumbe I). These two levels are sometimes categorised as gentry. Above the gentry are five levels of the peerage carrying the generic address of 'Lord'. So, for example the earl of Mount Edgcumbe would be correctly addressed as Lord Mount Edgcumbe.

The five ranks of the peerage in ascending order are **barons** (not to be confused with baronets), **viscounts, earls, marquesses,** and **dukes.** The oldest and most senior dukedom is that of the duchy of Cornwall, first created in 1337 and currently held by Prince Charles as the eldest son of the sovereign. Sir Richard Edgcumbe V was raised to the peerage with the rank of baron in 1742; his son Lord George Edgcumbe was promoted up a level to viscount in 1781 and up a further level again to earl in 1789. All these three titles were then held concurrently by subsequent earls. So for example, Queen Victoria's host in 1846, Lord Ernest Augustus Mount Edgcumbe, was the third earl but also the third viscount and the fifth baron.

When Lord George Edgcumbe entered the peerage, its ranks were hereditary with titles passed on to the next heir in the family. New legislation in 1958 however enabled the creation of life peers (non-hereditary) with the rank of baron (or baroness). Life peers now form the great majority of peers sitting in the house of lords and hereditary peers are being phased out. The last hereditary peer to be created was ex-prime minister Harold Macmillan as earl of Stockton in 1984. Sir Winston Churchill famously (twice) refused a dukedom.

In the gentry the creation of new baronetcies ceased in 1964. The sole exception has been Denis Thatcher (husband of prime minister Margaret Thatcher) who was made a hereditary baronet in 1990. New life knighthoods (non-hereditary) and the equivalent damehoods for women are awarded every year for exceptional acheivement or sevice in all walks of life and announced in the Queen's Honours lists published at New Year and on the queen's official birthday in June.

Dick Edgcumbe (as he was known to friends) was a notorious gambler and because of his reputation as the family black sheep, his portrait had put been put away out of sight in the cellar[12]. As a happy consequence it was saved and is on show today in Mount Edgcumbe House.

Dick the gambler became the second baron on his father's death in 1758. He had four children with a mistress called Ann Franks Day[13] but died a bachelor in his forties and was followed by his brother George.

There is a portrait in Mount Edgcumbe House of the brothers together as children. As a younger son, George (1721-1795) did not expect to inherit and joined the royal navy as a midshipman. By the 1770s he was an admiral and the commander-in-chief Plymouth. When a Spanish fleet threatened Plymouth in 1779 during the American Revolutionary War he felled dozens of ancient oak trees at Mount Edgcumbe to make way for gun emplacements. (Spain sided with America and against Britain in this war). His reward for sacrificing

21. The third earl, Ernest Augustus, was Queen Victoria's host at Mount Edgcumbe in 1846. (The Box, Plymouth/Mount Edgcumbe Collection)

the trees was promotion in rank from baron to viscount when George III and Queen Charlotte visited Mount Edgcumbe in 1781, and from viscount to earl when they visited again (and went to Cotehele) in 1789.

Victoria's host when she visited Mount Edgcumbe on 22 August 1846 was the third earl of Mount Edgcumbe, Ernest Augustus (1797-1861). His portrait hangs in the central hall of the house opposite that of his wife Caroline with their two young children – William Henry

Queen Victoria's childhood

Queen Victoria's father died when she was only eight months old. The family were economising by spending the winter away from London, in Sidmouth on the coast in Devon, when the duke of Kent caught a chill out walking, developed pneumonia, and died on 23 January 1820.

Edward's death left the duchess of Kent and her daughter in a precarious situation. The duke had been heavily in debt and the duchess had to renounce any interest in his estate in favour of his creditors. The duchess was in a strange country where she did not speak the language and wanted to return home to Germany. However, she was advised by her brother Prince Leopold of Saxe-Coburg, who was still living in England as the widower of Princess Charlotte, that it was vital for her daughter, as the future queen, to be brought up in Britain. He helped the duchess financially and she moved back to Kensington Palace where the young Victoria was brought up.

It was unfortunate that during Victoria's childhood her mother came under the influence of the comptroller of her household, called Sir John Conroy. Speculation at the time and since is that the two were lovers. Sir John saw an opportunity to be 'the power behind the throne' should little Victoria become queen while still a minor with her mother as the regent. He devised a restricted system of upbringing to isolate Victoria from the royal family, make Victoria dependent on her mother, and promote her mother as the prime candidate for regent. It was called 'The Kensington System'.

Victoria's uncle King William IV was at loggerheads with the duchess over Victoria's upbringing and seclusion from his court. He offered Victoria an independent income when she came of age at eighteen, but she was forced to refuse in terms dictated by her mother and Sir John. The king had no desire to see the duchess as regent, and just managed to stave this off. Victoria was eighteen on 24 May 1837; William IV died a month later, on 20 June. Victoria was queen and Sir John Conroy's hopes of power were over. His misguided attempts to control her childhood had the unhappy effect of alienating Victoria from her mother. But he also forged the resolute character that would serve Victoria well as queen.

(born in 1832) and his little sister Ernestine (born 1843). Countess Caroline was a lady-in-waiting to Victoria until forced to resign due to her husband's ill health. The earl was an invalid and crippled by gout. A suite of rooms on the ground floor was adapted for him at Mount Edgcumbe House; later he moved to a custom-built villa across the water in East Stonehouse (subsequently turned into a nursing home)[14].

Victoria wrote how it was a pleasure to be at Mount Edgcumbe again. She first mentioned it in her journal for August 1836 when she came to Plymouth with her mother, and she visited with Albert during the maiden voyage of the *Victoria and Albert* in August 1843.

... went in our Barge, proceeding to Mount Edgcumbe, ... which is the most lovely place imaginable. ... Drove first a little way up the hill and then through the Flower Garden ... full of the rarest evergreens and southern plants in the greatest beauty. After this we took, really a most splendid drive, all along the coast, winding above the Bay, to a great height, from which

22. Countess Caroline (wife of Ernst Augustus) with their two young children – William Henry (the future fourth earl) and his little sister Ernestine. (The Box, Plymouth/ Mount Edgcumbe Collection)

we had the most beautiful view ... – each turn of the road seemingly finer than the others. ... It is too lovely to attempt to describe.[15]

On the death of Earl Ernest Augustus in 1861 his son William Henry (1832-1917) became the fourth earl of Mount Edgcumbe. The widowed Countess Caroline retired with her daughter Ernestine to the east range (or wing) at Cotehele where some of their rooms are now included on the tour. As viscount Valletort (the title of the eldest son of the earl), William Henry was chosen by Prince Albert as one of three young men of exemplary character to be equerries to his son when sixteen-year-old Bertie was given his own establishment at White Lodge, Richmond in 1858. Victoria wrote that Valletort was '... an excellent, amiable, gentlemanlike young man ...'[16].

You might think setting up a separate household was to allow Bertie some independence now he was growing up, but he was effectively under house arrest. William Henry and the other equerries were given detailed instructions on how to behave; suitable subjects for conversation with the prince; even what to wear[17]! Fortunately, the affable Bertie bore no grudge and the two men became friends. William Henry went on to have a notable career as a royal courtier. He was lord of the bedchamber to Bertie (the male equivalent of lady-in-waiting) from 1862 to 1879 and held the senior positions of lord chamberlain (1879-1880) and lord steward (1885-1892) to Queen Victoria.

William Henry was married to Countess Katherine (called Katie by Victoria in her journal). They had three daughters in a row followed by an only son. Piers Alexander known as Alec in the family was born in 1865. There is a photograph in Mount Edgcumbe House of the three little girls cuddling their new-born baby brother. In another photograph Countess Katie looks drawn and unwell. She died young of consumption (tuberculosis) in 1874. During William Henry's long widowhood his sister Ernestine acted as hostess at Mount Edgcumbe. Ernestine was a bridesmaid at the wedding of Princess Helena (third daughter of Queen Victoria) in 1866 but never married herself. Eventually in 1906, William Henry married for a second time. His new wife was his widowed cousin Caroline, the daughter of his father's younger brother. The marriage was not long-lived; Countess Caroline died in 1909. A majestic portrait of William Henry later in life wearing his earl's robes hangs on the gallery of the central hall in Mount Edgcumbe House.

Chart 6 shows how the earls of Mount Edgcumbe ran out of direct heirs. William Henry (died 1917) was the last earl to be followed to

23. Earl William Henry and his second wife Countess Caroline with their dog Pepper photographed in the doorway to the Tudor Hall at Cotehele.

the title by his son. The inheritance then went sideways (in the same generation) with negative consequences for inheritance taxes. (This was because there are fewer years between the deaths on which taxes were charged.) The fifth earl Piers Alexander (1865-1944) had no children, and his heir was his second cousin Kenelm (1873-1965); their grandfathers had been brothers. The two men were similar in age and agreed that the estate should bypass Kenelm and go directly to his son[18]. Piers Richard (1914-1940) was the youngest of Kenelm's four children and the only son. A poem (possibly written by his mother) reveals huge relief when he was born in the early weeks of World War I.

> We watched and waited through the fleeting years
> In anxious hope that thou woulds't seal our joy;
> When Lo! Through parting clouds the Sun appears
> To bring, mid War's alarms, a strong limbed British boy![19]

Piers Richard Edgcumbe was killed in action on 27 May 1940 during the retreat from Dunkirk in World War II. Next in line (after his father Kenelm) was now yet another cousin who was a sheep farmer in New Zealand (chart 6).

More tragedy struck when Mount Edgcumbe House was destroyed by fire on the night of 22 March 1941 during the Plymouth Blitz. When an incendiary bomb landed on the roof there was not enough pressure to pump water up and extinguish the fire. The water mains had been damaged in a bombing raid the night before. The incendiary bomb burned through the roof and crashed into the house. The interior was completely burnt out and only fragments of the walls left standing. The family were forced to move once again to Cotehele. Kenelm's granddaughter, then a child, remembered 'No electricity ... Spooky nooks and crannies behind the tapestries ... The darkly cold stone steps winding up to our favourite Tower playground ...'[20].

Kenelm was seventy-one years old when he inherited the title as the sixth earl of Mount Edgcumbe in 1944. He faced the daunting prospect of maintaining two great houses, one an 'antique manor house' (Cotehele); the other a 'smoking ruin' (Mount Edgcumbe)[21]. Despite his advanced age the earl was committed to the restoration of Mount Edgcumbe House. In 1947 he gave Cotehele to the National Trust in lieu of inheritance taxes and in memory of his son Piers Richard, the Edgcumbe heir who gave his life for his country at Dunkirk. The transfer was assisted by funding from the *National Land Fund* set up in 1946 to help acquire important cultural assets for the nation as a memorial to the dead of World War II[22].

24. Mount Edgcumbe today, rebuilt by Earl Kenelm in the local red stone.

In 1958 the restoration of Mount Edgcumbe House began funded by war damage compensation monies. A decision was taken not to demolish the ruins and start again but to incorporate the surviving fragments of wall into the rebuild. Another decision was not to paint the exterior walls in white. In historic pictures Mount Edgcumbe

House is always shown as white in colour but today the walls are red (the colour of the local red stone with which the house is built). The new Mount Edgcumbe House resembles the original Tudor building in shape and design. The compensation monies did not stretch to rebuilding the West Wing where Queen Victoria had sat in the Gallery after lunch on her visit in August 1846 and sketched the view of the sea. The West Wing was a later addition to the original Tudor building and was enlarged in the early 1840s, not long before Victoria's visit. Where the West Wing once stood is now a small knot garden with a parterre of topiary and low box hedging. The interior of Mount Edgcumbe was restored in eighteenth-century style and furnished entirely with furniture, paintings, and works of art from the Edgcumbe family collection. These contents are still in the house today and a great part of its charm. The rooms are elegant, spacious, light-filled, and harmonious. Our guide told us how many visitors comment that this feels like a house they could live in.

25. The interior of Mount Edgcumbe was restored in eighteenth century style.

Earl Kenelm lived to see the work finished – but did not have long to enjoy it. His wife Countess Lillian died in 1964 and the earl in 1965. A portrait of the earl and countess together wearing their coronation robes (for the coronation of Queen Elizabeth II) dominates the central hall of the house they restored (illustration 16). It was a great achievement. The chapel on the first floor of Mount Edgcumbe House is dedicated to the memory of the sixth earl, his countess, and their only son.

After Kenelm's death the title passed to the New Zealand branch of the family descended from the younger brother of Victoria's host, Earl Ernest Augustus (chart 6). The seventh earl, Edward Piers (1903-1982), was already in his sixties when he inherited and moved to Mount Edgcumbe from New Zealand. To protect the estate from more inheritance taxes and secure its future, Mount Edgcumbe was sold to Cornwall County Council and Plymouth City Council in 1971. Their joint purchase reflects that Mount Edgcumbe has always been closely connected with Plymouth just across the water. Indeed, this 'forgotten corner of Cornwall' was in Devon (not Cornwall) until the county boundary was redrawn in 1844.

The dynastic failure of the earls of Mount Edgcumbe to have sons continued. Edward Piers and his wife were childless, and the next earl was his nephew Robert (1939-2021). The eighth earl caused something of a scandal when he came to Mount Edgcumbe from New Zealand without his wife and formed a new relationship with a local barmaid (they eventually married)[23]. Mount Edgcumbe has a fine collection of family portraits and one of my favourites was that of Earl Robert. He sports a white dinner jacket with multi-coloured bow tie and looks as though he is ready to join the party. The earl split his time between Mount Edgcumbe and New Zealand, and his portrait includes a kiwi bird representing his New Zealand links. Earl Robert was the last earl to live in Mount Edgcumbe House. When he moved out (to nearby Empacombe House) in 1987 the house became a museum. The earl had five daughters with his first wife but no son and on his death in

June 2021 the title passed to his half-brother (from his father's second marriage) Christopher, born in 1950, who lives in New Zealand[24].

After our guided tour of Mount Edgcumbe House my husband and I walked down the ancient avenue of trees to explore Mount Edgcumbe Country Park. The eight hundred and sixty-five acres of the park are a delight to visit, criss-crossed with walking paths, dotted with monuments and follies, and with incredible views from its ten miles of coastline. There is so much to see that you must allow plenty of time! What is special is that this park was developed over centuries by generations of the same family. The Deer Garden at the visitor centre was opened by Earl Robert in 2015 to celebrate five hundred years since his ancestor Sir Piers Edgcumbe first enclosed a deer park at Mount Edgcumbe in 1515. The deer grazing in the deer park today are descendants of that original herd.

The Bowling Green next to the beach at Barn Pool (where Victoria's royal yacht was moored) dates from around 1670, when the son of Colonel Sir Piers Edgcumbe III held the inheritance. There was a Civil War re-enactment on the Bowling Green the day we visited with musketeers in period costume firing off demonstration muskets. A walk along Earl's Drive (an eighteenth-century driveway for carriages through the park) took us past an artificial ruined tower called The Folly built by Lord Richard Edgcumbe I after he was promoted from the ranks of the gentry in 1742 ('sham' ruins were a popular feature of eighteenth-century gardens). Further along the coastline at Penlee Point is Queen Adelaide's Grotto; a grand look-out fashioned from an old cliff cave and named for the wife of King William IV. William and Adelaide stayed at Mount Edgcumbe in 1827 (before William's accession to the throne).

As a keen amateur gardener, the highlight of the park for me was the suite of themed gardens next to the water at the Cremyll entrance. These beautiful gardens are laid out as distinct and separate garden 'rooms' and protected from the sea and the harsh east winds by a Great Hedge of evergreen oak (quercus ilex) over thirty feet high (ten metres) originally planted around 1700. The English Garden with cool lawns and magnificent magnolia trees dates from around 1770; the French Garden with geometric beds and blazing carpet bedding from 1803. The Orangery in the gracious Italian Garden was built to house orange trees brought back from Constantinople by Dick Edgcumbe (the second baron) in the 1740s. Already an addicted gambler he was packed off to Turkey by the family for seven years in an attempt to keep him out of trouble!

When Cornwall County Council and Plymouth City Council acquired the Mount Edgcumbe estate in 1971 these inspiring garden rooms were dilapidated and overgrown. A huge amount of work has been done since then to rescue and regenerate them. The American Garden was added in 1989 to commemorate the American soldiers who left for D-Day from Barn Pool beach in June 1944. The Jubilee Garden marks Queen Elizabeth II's golden jubilee in 2002; the Relic Garden

26. Cotehele Quay, where Victoria landed, in the early morning mist.

made in 2011 (my favourite) features fragments of old stonework and garden ornaments found discarded in the park. My husband and I wandered happily from garden room to room enjoying one surprise after another. The biggest surprise was that (apart from the popular Italian garden where the Orangery is now a café) we saw no other visitors. We ended our tour of garden rooms in the Fern Dell, pet cemetery for the Edgcumbe family for two hundred years. First to be buried here was Cupid (died 1789) the pet pig of Countess Emma, wife of the first earl. Countess Emma was an eccentric who was devoted to Cupid. She is said to have taken her pet pig everywhere including to the dinner table[25]!

As I was writing the final words of this chapter my husband and I revisited Cotehele. We parked at Cotehele Quay and walked along the bank of the Tamar to find a small ancient building in the trees called *the Chapel in the Woods*. This was built in 1490 by Sir Richard Edgcumbe I, the founder of the Edgcumbe family fortunes, to mark the site of his narrow escape from the agents of Richard III. This is where the story of the Edgcumbes and their two great houses, Cotehele and Mount Edgcumbe, all began. Cotehele House and Mount Edgcumbe House are open to the public in the summer months; their gardens and grounds are open all year round. Both properties are blessed with welcoming and helpful staff and provide an excellent visitor experience.

5.

ST MICHAEL'S MOUNT AND KYNANCE COVE

There was a special moment when the royal yacht *Victoria and Albert* steamed into Mount's Bay near Penzance in south-west Cornwall on the royal tour in 1846. Queen Victoria wrote in her journal how the sun lit up the island called St Michael's Mount. The Mount is one of the iconic sights of Cornwall. The small steep rocky island with its fairy-tale castle on the peak dominates the broad sweep of the bay. St Michael's Mount captured my imagination when I first saw it as a child and still takes my breath away however many times I go there. There are many stunning photographs of St Michael's Mount taken in all tides and weathers, including that at high tide in illustration 27. But to my mind no photograph can truly capture its magic and you must come and see St Michael's Mount for yourself. Map 4 shows Mount's Bay and the location of St Michael's Mount close to the village of Marazion.

St Michael's Mount was purchased by Colonel John St Aubyn (1610-1684) in 1659 and belonged to the St Aubyn family until it was donated to the National Trust in 1954. The family retained a long lease on a wing of the castle and still live on the island and operate the visitor business. St Michael's Mount is a tidal island and visiting is quite an adventure.

27. St Michael's Mount at high tide showing the submerged causeway in the foreground. (Miraphoto/Shutterstock)

At low tide visitors walk out to the Mount along a paved causeway laid over a shingle bank by Lord John first baron St Levan (1829-1908) in 1898. At high tide the only access is by water. A fleet of small boats plies to and fro between the village of Marazion on the mainland and the small harbour on the Mount. This harbour was built in 1727 by Sir John St Aubyn III (1700-1744), the third of six baronets before they were elevated to the peerage as barons St Levan in 1887. Very confusingly five of the six baronets and three of the five barons (to date) all have had the same first name of John! Chart 7 lists the St Aubyns at St Michael's Mount. I have used numbering (roman numerals) to help distinguish the baronets and barons of the same first name.

When Victoria visited St Michael's Mount with Prince Albert on the morning of Sunday 6 September 1846, they came by water in the royal barge. A brass plaque inlaid into the granite at the top of the harbour steps records where the queen stepped ashore. In the shape of a small footprint, it carries the initials VR (Victoria Regina). Victoria was short (around five feet or one and a half metres) and her footprint is quite tiny. Next to it in the harbour wall, a larger plaque gives details of her visit. Further along the quay are more footprints marking the visit of Victoria's great-great-granddaughter Queen Elizabeth II with her husband Prince Philip in 2013. Most visitors hurry past the footprints heading for the small village at the end of the quay with visitor centre, shop, and cafe. The village was revamped by Lord John St Levan I when he carried out major rebuilding works and added a new wing to the castle from 1873. To see the castle visitors must scramble up a steep and potentially treacherous rocky slope. St Michael's Mount website warns that 'some parts of the island can be tricky to navigate' and paths 'are steep, cobbled and uneven with no handrails in some places'[1]. I consoled myself with the thought that Victoria, burdened with long skirts and heavy clothes, had made the climb before me. And it was well worth the effort when we arrived at the top.

St Michael's Mount is named for the Archangel St Michael protector of heaven against the forces of evil. There is an old Cornish legend that St Michael appeared to local fisherman in AD 495 standing high above the sea on the Mount. A modern bronze statue in the castle church shows St Michael defeating Lucifer (the devil). With one arm the saint holds his sword on high, with the other he offers the hand of mercy to a repulsive looking Lucifer who cowers at his feet. St Michael is the patron of churches in high places and another vision of the saint led to the foundation of the abbey of Mont St Michel on another tidal island just across the English Channel in Normandy. Mont St Michel translates as St Michael's Mount.

After the Norman invasion of 1066, William the Conqueror gave much of Cornwall (including St Michael's Mount) to his half-brother Robert Count of Mortain. Count Robert had carried the banner of St Michael in the decisive Battle of Hastings. Around 1080 Count Robert granted St Michael's Mount to the Benedictine Abbey of Mont St Michel. The French abbots established a small priory on the Cornish Mount and built the church consecrated in 1144.

Victoria and Albert

Queen Victoria and Prince Albert were married at the Chapel Royal, St James's Palace in London on 10 February 1840 when they were both twenty years old. The couple were first cousins and chart 1 shows their family relationship. The marriage was arranged by Albert's family, and they hardly knew each other before the wedding. Perhaps it is not surprising that their first years together were stormy given their different characters and expectations of the marriage. For Victoria the wedding was the result of a whirlwind romance. She fell passionately in love at first sight when Albert arrived at Windsor Castle on inspection as her intended bridegroom in October 1839. Her devotion to Albert would never waver but she could be very difficult to live with. Victoria had inherited some of her Hanoverian predecessors' worst character traits. She could be warm and loving, but also obstinate, emotional, and self-centred.

For Albert on the other hand, being the husband of Queen Victoria was his career. From childhood Albert had been brought up in the expectation of marrying his cousin Victoria. Albert's temperament was more reserved, cool, and logical. He never did anything without carefully thinking it through and was horrified by his wife's emotional outbursts. Victoria was prone to create scenes and then Albert would retreat from her, wait for things to cool down, and put his side of the case in writing.

Albert's induction into the British royal family had not been easy. Victoria's choice of bridegroom was not popular with the British people who generally took the view that she could have done a good deal better for herself than a second son from a minor German duchy. As the husband of a female sovereign Albert was in an unusual and somewhat difficult position. A princess marrying the king of Great Britain would have automatically been granted the title of queen, but Victoria's attempts to obtain the title of king for Albert were firmly rebuffed by her government. There were no helpful precedents to inform his role as male consort. Of the previous three queens regnant, Queen Elizabeth I was unmarried; Queen Mary II deferred to her husband (King William III) who was joint sovereign; and Queen Anne's husband (*Prince George of Denmark*) seemed largely happy to remain in the background. Albert was not content to live the leisured lifestyle of a wealthy prince but wanted to be of service to his new country.

Albert understood his role was to support his wife in her public position as head of state, but he expected to have a guiding role as her chief adviser and to be head of the family in their private life. He had studied diligently to be able to help Victoria by sharing her duties as queen. But Victoria still revelled in the freedom and independence she had gained on succeeding to the throne in 1837 at the age of eighteen. She positively did not want Albert's help. She continued to see her ministers alone and refused to show him any official papers. Albert found the situation hard to deal with and complained that 'I am only the husband and not the master in the house'[2].

28. Queen Victoria and Prince Albert as newlyweds.

But it was Albert who emerged dominant in the relationship. Victoria was desperately in love with her husband and ready to give way. By the mid-1840s the worst of their marital storms were over. Albert learned to manage his wife's more volatile character although dealing with Victoria's emotional outbursts would always be a strain. From now on his role as consort would grow until he was effectively joint monarch. Victoria came to rely on him in everything, and this would later be a real issue in her inability to cope with his early death.

The link with Mont St Michel weakened during the long war between England and France, called the Hundred Years' War (1337-1453), over rights of succession to the French throne. In 1414 Henry V expropriated St Michael's Mount from the Abbey of Mont St Michel and gave it instead to his new religious foundation at Syon Abbey in Middlesex. The Mount was part of Syon Abbey when both were dissolved by Henry VIII in 1539 during the Reformation following the annulment of his marriage to Catherine of Aragon.

The Museum Room in the castle on St Michael's Mount displays a collection of paintings illustrating important events in its history. One of the most romantic, and intriguing, is the stay here of Lady Catherine Gordon, wife of a pretender to the throne. In September 1497, during the reign of Henry VII, the pretender landed in Cornwall not far from St Michael's Mount, claiming to be the rightful king of England. Cornwall was already seething with discontent. Earlier in the year Henry VII had imposed higher taxes to pay for a potential war with Scotland. The fiercely independent Cornish saw no reason why they should pay for hostilities in a faraway part of the kingdom. It was not so many years since Henry VII had won the crown by defeating Richard III at the Battle of Bosworth Field (1485) at the end of the Wars of the Roses. There were still some who would have preferred a king from the House of York, rather than the Lancastrian Henry. The taxes revolt had been put down by the king's troops but now the Cornish rose again in support of the pretender.

The pretender left his wife in the safety of St Michael's Mount and marched off to claim his throne. I can imagine her gazing at the incomparable views from the monastery windows and wondering if her husband would ever return (he did not). Lady Catherine Gordon was a Scottish aristocrat known as *The White Rose of Scotland* for her beauty and charm[3]. She was a distant connection of the king of Scotland who had arranged her marriage to the pretender. Whoever her husband really was he had maintained the pretence of royalty through years of living at several foreign courts (France, the Low Countries and

Scotland) where he was accepted as the rightful king of England. He claimed to be Richard Duke of York, the younger son of King Edward IV, who had miraculously escaped from imprisonment in the Tower of London. If true, this would have made him the Yorkist heir to the throne. But it was not true. Both nine-year-old Richard and his twelve-year-old brother Edward (briefly King Edward V) disappeared into the Tower when their uncle Richard III usurped the throne in 1483 and were almost certainly murdered soon after. The fate of the so-called *Princes in the Tower* is one of the great tragedies of royal history.

29. The Mount has a special microclimate and exotic plants flourish in its terraced gardens. (St Michael's Mount/Claire Braithwaite)

The pretender was proclaimed as King Richard IV in the Cornish town of Bodmin (see map 2). But his support began to dwindle as his Cornish followers marched further away from home. The pretender was no hero; faced with the news that Henry VII's army was approaching he deserted the remains of his army at Taunton in Somerset and was captured soon after. Under interrogation he confessed to being a Flemish merchant called Perkin Warbeck but is this the end of the pretender's story? His portrait bears a striking resemblance to his supposed father King Edward IV. Some historians have speculated that he might have been an illegitimate son of Edward IV, or of one of Edward's brothers, or indeed of his sister Margaret Duchess of Burgundy who enthusiastically welcomed him as her nephew Richard at the Hapsburg court in the Low Countries[4]. When Lady Catherine was told her husband had admitted to being a commoner called Perkin Warbeck, she loyally declared it was the man and not the king she loved[5]. Henry VII sent an escort to collect her from St Michael's Mount and she was detained under genteel house arrest at court as a lady-in-waiting to his wife, Elizabeth of York. The pretender was also treated leniently for a while before he was eventually eliminated as a potential threat and executed for treason in 1499.

After the dissolution of the monasteries in the reign of Henry VIII, St Michael's Mount was a military fortress to guard against threats from the sea. The first beacon to signal the approach of the Spanish Armada was lit on top of the church tower in 1588. Spanish ships landed in Mounts Bay in 1595 and burned the villages of Mousehole and Penzance. During the English Civil War (1642-1651) the roundhead Colonel John St Aubyn was appointed captain or military governor of St Michael's Mount following its capture from the royalists. In 1659 Colonel John purchased the Mount from the previous (royalist) owners and the era of St Aubyn ownership began. According to family tradition, Colonel John died by drowning when he was swept off the causeway attempting to cross from the mainland on his horse[6]. His son John (1645-1699) was created the first baronet St Aubyn in 1671.

Floorplans in the guidebook for St Michael's Mount show how over the centuries the old monastery and military barracks were converted to a stately home. The visitor tour begins in the Armoury and Entrance Hall in what was the military side of the castle (the west wing). Next door Sir John's Room (the study) is part of an extension built in the sixteenth century to join up the military wing with the rooms of the old monastery in the south wing. The monks' kitchen is now the library; their pantry is the smoking room; and the monks' refectory is a grand dining room delightfully named the Chevy Chase Room. Visitors sometimes ask if this is after the well-known American comic actor called Chevy Chase! In fact, both owe their names to an old English song called *The Ballad of Chevy Chase*. The room has a plaster frieze running round under the ceiling depicting hunting scenes based on the ballad; the actor was born Cornelius Chase and acquired the family nickname of Chevy because of the ballad[7]. *The Ballad of Chevy Chase* is about a hunting party (the Chase bit of the title) in the Cheviot Hills on the England/Scotland border (hence Chevy).

30. The Chevy Chase Room, named after a medieval ballad, was once the monks' refectory. (St Michael's Mount/Mike Newman)

In her journal account of her visit to St Michael's Mount, Victoria mentions the Chevy Chase Room frieze and says the castle '...must be a nice house to live in, there being a good many rooms & some very pretty ones, ...'[8]. She may have had in mind the Blue Drawing Rooms in mock-gothic style with Wedgwood blue walls and delicate white plasterwork. These two rooms (the Main Blue Drawing Room and the Small Blue Drawing Room) were converted from a ruined lady chapel by the fourth baronet, Sir John St Aubyn IV (1726-1772), and became the main reception space. Victoria was given tea by the housekeeper Mrs Thomasina Sims in the Main Blue Drawing Room (illustration 32) during her visit in 1846; the official photos were taken here when Queen Elizabeth II visited in 2013[9].

Victoria came to St Michael's Mount when there was no St Aubyn in residence following the long 'reign' of the fifth baronet[10]. Sir John St Aubyn V (1758-1839) inherited the title at fourteen and died aged eighty-two. Sir John V was multi-talented – a member of parliament; leading mineralogist; patron of the arts; and a great collector. He was also wildly extravagant and an inveterate gambler. An anecdote in the guidebook tells how in one night's play at his club Brooks's in London, he gambled away family property on which much of the London district of Putney was subsequently built[11]! The fifth baronet's private life was unconventional in that he did not marry until late in life and then his bride was not from the gentry. Sir John V lived for several years with Martha Nicholls, the daughter of an employee, with whom he had five illegitimate children before the relationship ended and she was comfortably pensioned off[12]. His lasting relationship was with the daughter of a farmer from Marazion called Juliana Vinicombe. They were together for forty-five years and eventually married in 1822 after their nine illegitimate children were grown up.

When Sir John V died heavily in debt and without a legitimate heir in 1839 it took several years to sort out the inheritance[13]. Under the law relating to illegitimacy the later marriage of Sir John V and Juliana did not legitimise their children. The St Aubyn baronetcy became extinct and the entailed family properties passed to a nephew. St Michael's Mount was inherited by Sir John V's eldest illegitimate son, James St Aubyn (1783-1862), the son of Martha Nicholls. James was succeeded by his younger half-brother Edward (1799-1872) for whom the baronetcy was recreated in 1866 during Victoria's reign.

The guidebook for the Mount is structured as a personal tour with the current baron (the fifth) Lord James St Levan (born in 1950). I really liked this personal touch. Lord James intersperses the history and descriptions of the rooms with family stories and memories of the Mount. His father remembered meals in the Chevy Chase Room being served by family footmen wearing canary

31. Sir James Aubyn V
had an unconventional private life.
(St Michael's Mount)

yellow livery; his uncle Giles (his father's younger brother) donated the Napoleon memorabilia displayed in the smoking room that includes part of the coat the French emperor wore at the Battle of Waterloo in 1815. Giles St Aubyn was a well-known historian who wrote notable biographies of both Queen Victoria and her son Bertie, King Edward VII[14]. Lord James and his wife moved to St Michael's Mount on the retirement to the mainland of the fourth baron (his uncle) in 2003. Their home is in the east wing of the castle. This was built from 1873 by Lord John St Levan I at the colossal cost (for the time) of one hundred thousand pounds[15]. It is difficult to state the equivalent in money terms today, but the ONS (Office of National Statistics) CPI (consumer prices index) calculator on the internet puts it at over eleven million pounds[16].

32. Queen Victoria took tea in the Blue Drawing Room
during her visit to St Michael's Mount. (St Michael's Mount/Mike Newman)

The east wing is a remarkable feat of architecture stretching down the hillside underneath the South Terrace of the castle. Visitors admiring the wonderful views from this terrace can hardly imagine they are standing on the roof of the St Aubyn family home. When seen from the mainland this Victorian extension to the old castle blends in so well it is hard to distinguish where the medieval monastery ends, and the east wing begins. A circular turret on the South Terrace leads to a staircase descending through all five floors of the St Aubyn home. In the guidebook Lord James explains how theirs is an upside-down house, with the bedrooms at the bottom and the cellar on the top floor. He tells how his children liked to use the terrace roof as a skateboard park after the visitors had gone home.

Lord James's grandfather, Lord Francis St Levan (1895-1978), donated St Michael's Mount to the National Trust in 1954 together with a large financial endowment to help maintain it. By the terms of the agreement, the St Aubyn family kept ownership of the east wing (a nine-hundred-and ninety-nine-year lease) and a license to run the visitor business. The Mount quickly became one of the National Trust's most popular attractions and hundreds of thousands of visitors come to the small tidal island each year. Opening hours in the winter months when the boat service does not operate are limited by the tides and by bad weather. Readers hoping to visit should check the website for up-to-date information.

While the royal flotilla was moored at St Michael's Mount, Albert went ashore at Penzance to visit the Wherrytown serpentine rock works. The prince brought back specimens of the rock for Bertie and ordered mantelpieces and pedestals for Osborne House. Serpentine is a form of marble quarried only on the Lizard peninsula at the eastern end of Mount's Bay (map 4). When polished the rock shows up attractive veins and variations in colour. On the afternoon of Sunday 6 September 1846, following the royal visit to St Michael's Mount, the royal yacht *Victoria and Albert* called in at Kynance Cove on the Lizard for Albert to see this Cornish marble in situ.

Kynance Cove has been a famous beauty spot since Victorian times and is described by the National Trust as 'a Cornish gem' and 'one of the world's most spectacular beaches'[17]. As my husband and I walked down the steep path from the cliff top the idyllic scenery of the cove came slowly into view. The pale blue of a summer sky merged into the deep blue of the sea and the crystal turquoise waters and white sands of the cove. Wow! This felt more like the Mediterranean than the English Channel! The tide was in, and the first bathers of the day were drifting in the shallow waters of the cove. At low tide there are serpentine rock islets, rock stacks and cliff caves to explore. I could quite see why Albert was enchanted by the scenery when he came ashore and sent a message for Victoria and their children to join him. Victoria recorded how they were 'rowed to the truly beautiful rocks, with caves and little creeks. On the coast were two little houses [now the café] and the place is called Kynance Cove.'[18]

Cornish Marble

Serpentine (or serpentinite) rock was formed millions of years ago when part of the Earth's mantle was forced up through the crust and exposed to seawater. The rock takes its name from its scaly, reptilian appearance streaked with veins. The Wherrytown factory at Penzance, opened around 1840, shipped the raw rock across Mount's Bay from quarries on the Lizard to produce polished slabs and carved decorative items such as columns, obelisks, urns, fireplaces, tombstones, and other ornamental pieces. By the time of Prince Albert's visit in 1846 there were reportedly thirty-seven employees[19].

Under Prince Albert's patronage serpentine pieces from the Wherrytown works were showcased at the Great Exhibition of 1851 held in the glittering Crystal Palace erected in Hyde Park in London. Albert was the driving force behind this magnificent and hugely successful showcase for British products and industry. A pair of thirteen feet high (four metres) serpentine obelisks from the Wherrytown factory were prize winners at the event[20]. Serpentine became fashionable and demand for the product soared. In 1853 a rival company was formed with a factory at Poltesco, Carleon Cove, on the eastern side of the Lizard. This had the advantage of working the serpentine onsite without the cost of shipping to Penzance.

But the Cornish marble bubble soon burst. The Lizard has a maritime climate and in other parts of the country the rock did not weather so well. The popularity of serpentine declined and imported foreign marbles took up the demand. The Wherrytown works closed in 1865 and Poltesco in 1893[21].

There are still small serpentine workshops on the Lizard producing beautiful souvenirs for tourists. There are examples of serpentine rock to see everywhere in this lesser-known part of Cornwall – in the cliffs at Kynance Cove, the tower at St Wynwallow's Church in Lizard village, in farm gateposts and the stiles on walking paths. In Grade church near Cadgwith we happened upon a magnificent carved and polished lectern made of red serpentine (the rarest and therefore most expensive type). This stunning example of the finished Victorian product was a gift from the manager of the Poltesco factory when the church was renovated in 1863[22].

33. Kynance Cove has been celebrated by artists and poets
for hundreds of years; this picture was painted in 1911.

Because of its fame Kynance Cove is exceptionally busy in the summer season. We arrived at eight thirty in the morning to claim the last remaining space in the car park. National Trust stewards had already marked out several surrounding fields to take the overflow. The cove is only accessible by a ten-minute walk down a steep path from the cliff top car park. If you can manage this walk the pure beauty of Kynance Cove makes it well worth a visit.

6.

PENDENNIS CASTLE
FALMOUTH AND
ST MAWES CASTLE

Queen Victoria's arrival in Falmouth on the royal yacht in September 1846 was greeted by a gun salute from the battery at Pendennis Castle. The garrison presented arms and the castle grounds were full of cheering spectators. In their coverage of the queen's visit *The Illustrated London News* published a poem referring to the role of Pendennis in England's history (see extract overleaf). The castle was built by Henry VIII to protect the harbour against attack by his foreign enemies and saw its finest hour upholding the rights of Charles I against his enemies in parliament. Pendennis was the last stand of the royalist army in the west during the English Civil War (1642-1651) and the scene of two dramatic royal escapes from the clutches of the parliamentarians. Situated on a rocky headland above the town of Falmouth, Pendennis now provided the backdrop for the visit of a queen.

A famous incident in the boyhood of the future King Edward VII took place while the royal yacht was in the harbour at Falmouth. There was huge interest in Victoria and Albert's four-year-old son during the royal visit to Cornwall. Little Prince Albert Edward (always called

Bertie in the family) was roundly cheered by crowds of well-wishers whenever he appeared. As the eldest son of the reigning sovereign Bertie was the duke of Cornwall from his birth on 9 November 1841. He was created the prince of Wales only one month later. Bertie was the twenty-first duke of Cornwall since the duchy was created in 1337 but only the third known to have visited Cornwall. His arrival on the royal tour in 1846 was the first time a duke of Cornwall had been in Cornwall since the future Charles II (the sixteenth duke of Cornwall) fled from Pendennis Castle to France two hundred years before during the English Civil War!

Arrival at Falmouth

Hark! from old Falmouth's rocky shore
The shouts still echo to the ear,
Pendennis lends its cannons' roar
Commingled with the people's cheer.

And surely since that glorious day*
Rarely the Cornwall coast hath seen
More joy and festival display
Than that which lately hail'd the Queen.[1]

*A reference to the defeat of the Spanish Armada in 1588.

The mayor and town councillors from Penryn (a small port five miles upstream) went aboard the royal yacht at Falmouth on the morning of Monday 7 September 1846, to present an address of welcome to the queen. They also made a special request and asked to meet the duke of Cornwall. Victoria brought her young son out on deck where he was introduced by the Foreign Secretary Lord Palmerston (travelling as part of Victoria's entourage). This moment is depicted in an artist's impression (illustration 34) published at the end of Victoria's reign[2].

34. The duke of Cornwall (Bertie) meets the mayor
and town councillors of Penryn.

The mayor of Penryn said he hoped the young prince would grow up to be a blessing to his parents and the country. It seems unlikely that in later years his mother would have agreed he did. When her beloved husband Albert died aged only forty-two in 1861, Victoria blamed their son Bertie for his father's death. The worsening of Albert's last illness coincided with finding out about his son's loss of virginity to an actress. In forty years of waiting for the throne, Bertie undertook many public engagements that Victoria refused to carry out but was never given any worthwhile role by his mother, against the advice of her prime ministers. Instead, Bertie devoted himself to pleasure and high living, earning the nicknames of *Tum Tum* and *Edward the Caresser*.

Pendennis Castle and its twin St Mawes Castle on the other side of the river Fal estuary were built by King Henry VIII (1491-1547) in the 1540s as part of a chain of coastal defences along the south and east coasts of England. Both castles are now English Heritage properties.

Bertie

In September 1846 Bertie was four years old and already something of a disappointment to his parents. He was not as intelligent or studious as his sister Vicky who was a year older. His governess thought Bertie was 'shy and timid, with very good principles, and particularly an exact observer of truth'[3]. But Bertie was burdened from the start by a heavy weight of unrealistic parental expectations. Victoria and Albert were just desperate that Bertie should take after his strait-laced and hardworking father and not after her degenerate Hanoverian uncles (or indeed Albert's philandering father and brother). Victoria was already expressing these feelings in a letter to her uncle (King Leopold of Belgium) three weeks after Bertie's birth[4].

With high ideas in mind, Albert devised an impossibly ambitious plan of education for his son. Bertie's days were to be filled with lessons and worthy pursuits with little time for leisure or amusements. Albert was warned that such a system if carried out too young would overtax the brain of a bright boy and 'induce inevitable disgust' of education in a slow one[5]. Not surprisingly poor Bertie constantly failed to measure up and was sometimes driven by frustration to temper and tantrums. When Bertie was six the diarist Charles Greville confided to his diary 'the queen says he is a stupid boy' and '... the hereditary and unfailing antipathy of our Sovereigns to their Heirs Apparent seems thus early to be taking root, and the Queen does not much like the child.'[6] This was a reference to the recurring pattern of previous Hanoverian kings being on extremely bad terms with their sons and heirs.

In the royal nursery Vicky took the limelight and put Bertie in the shade. Highly intelligent and precocious from the start, Vicky was always her father's favourite child. (Victoria's favourite child would be her fourth son Arthur born in 1850.) She completely overshadowed Bertie and no wonder (until the succession was explained) that he assumed Vicky would follow their mother as queen[7]. It is a tribute to his innate good nature that Bertie always remained fond of his sister. Bertie's genial nature and people skills would make him very popular with the British public and a far better king than either of his parents might have imagined when he succeeded as King Edward VII in 1901.

Following his break with the church of Rome and the annulment in 1533 of his marriage to Catherine of Aragon, Henry VIII was in an exposed position internationally. The king's main rivals in Europe were King Francis I of France and the Holy Roman Emperor Charles V (ruler of Germany, Belgium, and the Netherlands; and also the king of Spain). Charles was Catherine's nephew and had vigorously defended his aunt's rights. Francis I and Charles V were at war with each other until they signed a truce in 1538[8]. It now looked likely they could combine forces and invade England on the urging of the pope to reinstate Catholicism.

35. Pendennis Castle with Falmouth and the Carrick Roads in the background. (Shutterstock/Tim Woolcock Photography)

Henry VIII reacted quickly to the threat and built new fortifications along the coastline to protect his vulnerable harbours and anchorages from French and Spanish fleets. One important harbour was the sheltered waters of the Carrick Roads (the estuary of the river Fal – see map 5) in west Cornwall. Blockhouses to mount canon were built on either side of the estuary to pour crossfire on any enemy ships trying to enter. From 1540 these defences were developed into the twin Henrician castles of Pendennis and St Mawes. The original blockhouses became part of the castles' wider defences and are still there today.

Henry VIII's new castles at Pendennis and St Mawes were purpose-built artillery forts to house canon and never intended to be royal residences. Their layout consisted of a circular keep or gun tower, housing rudimentary accommodation for the artillery crew as well as the gun platforms, surrounded by lower bastions to provide extra fire power. Pendennis has a single bastion (or chemise) in a circle around the gun tower whilst St Mawes has three semi-circular bastions (or lunettes) in a trefoil or clover leaf pattern. St Mawes was embellished with decorative carved stonework and, rather unusually, Latin inscriptions in praise of Henry VIII and his young son, later King Edward VI (1537-1553). These flattering comments were possibly an attempt to curry favour with the king by Thomas Treffry of Place House Fowey (see chapter 7) who supervised the building of St Mawes Castle and became its first deputy governor. In translation from the Latin, the inscriptions on the three bastions read

Henry VIII, most excellent king of England, France and Ireland.
Rejoice happy Cornwall now that Edward is duke. [The king's son Edward was the duke of Cornwall.]
May Edward resemble his father in fame and deeds.[9]

St Mawes Castle was built close to the shoreline and looks its best from the sea. In her journal Victoria records that she sketched St Mawes Castle from the royal yacht while it was moored in Falmouth Harbour[10]. Both she and Albert were accomplished artists and sketching was a favourite pastime. St Mawes Castle is a two mile walk along the coastal path from my Cornish home and I visit regularly. It is a tranquil spot even in the height of the busy summer season. I like to sit in the grounds to gaze at the beautiful sea views and watch the gaily-coloured foot-passenger ferries nipping back and forth to Falmouth and Pendennis Castle. A popular local event each year to raise money for the RNLI (Royal National Lifeboat Institution) is the *Castle 2 Castle* open water swim. Scores of hardy competitors enter the sea at Pendennis Castle and swim the one-mile distance across the Carrick Roads to come ashore at St Mawes Castle.

36. St Mawes Castle around the time of Victoria's visit.

However, St Mawes' idyllic location close to the shore meant it suffered from a serious design flaw. Built with rising ground behind it, the castle was near impossible to defend from an attack by land. In *The Survey of Cornwall* (published 1602/1603) Richard Carew commented that

Saint Mawes lieth lower and better to annoy shipping, but Pendennis standeth higher and stronger to defend itself.[11]

When Parliament laid siege to both castles in 1646 during the English Civil War St Mawes surrendered without a shot being fired whereas Pendennis held out for five months. Pendennis became the more

37. Henry VIII built Pendennis and St Mawes castles as part of a chain of coastal defences.

important of the two castles strategically. St Mawes remained largely unchanged and looks much the same today as in Tudor times.

The invasion scares of 1538 (that led to the twin castles being built) did not materialise but there were later threats. Increasing tensions led to war with Spain in 1585 (the Anglo-Spanish War 1585-1604) and the Cornish Coast was harried by Spanish ships based across the English Channel in Brittany. The Great Armada sailed past the Carrick Roads in 1588 (only to come to grief further up the Channel) but in 1596 another huge fleet set off from Spain intending to occupy Pendennis as a bridgehead to invade the rest of England[12]. Fortuitous gale force winds meant that this later armada never got further than Land's End! To counter the threat of Spanish invasion Pendennis was strengthened between 1597 and 1600 (during the reign of Henry VIII's daughter Queen Elizabeth I) by an extensive system of outer bastions and ramparts. Bombardment by parliamentary forces during the siege of Pendennis in the Civil War failed to breach these strong defences. Starvation forced Pendennis to surrender.

Henry VIII appointed John Killigrew (died 1567) as the first governor of Pendennis. The castle was built on Killigrew land, and three generations of the family held the governorship until John

Killigrew III (1554-1605) was sacked in 1598 for piracy and other nefarious activities. He is supposed to have taken a bribe to surrender Pendennis to the Spanish[13]. The Killigrew home was Arwenack on the Falmouth waterfront below Pendennis. They were a colourful family, both famous as the founders of the town of Falmouth and notorious for their activities as pirates out of the nearby Helford River. 'For pyratts and rovers they have byn commonly known', said an early history[14]. Piracy and smuggling were widespread in sea-faring Cornwall, with so-say respectable gentlemen routinely taking part. It was a fine line to draw between heroic privateering (plundering foreign ships in time of war) and criminal piracy (plundering foreign ships when not at war). The crown sanctioned the former and sometimes turned an official blind eye to the latter.

Chart 8 has a genealogy for the Killigrews of Arwenack. John Killigrew was succeeded as the governor of Pendennis by his son, John Killigrew II (died 1584). John II was knighted by Queen Elizabeth I but (like his father) spent time in prison for piracy. In what seems an extraordinary turn of events given his own involvement, John II was appointed chairman of a commission to investigate piracy in Cornwall. John II and his wife were suspected when a Spanish ship moored in harbour off Arwenack was boarded and plundered with the crew thrown overboard. Strange to say the commission took no action! Their son John III, the third governor of Pendennis, was deeply involved in piracy and ended his days in prison[15].

The town of Falmouth was founded by the sons of John III and did not exist when Pendennis Castle was built. Sir John Killigrew IV (1583-1633) began the development of a small hamlet next to Arwenack; his brother Sir Peter Killigrew (1593-1667) obtained a charter for the new town of Falmouth in 1661 from the newly restored King Charles II. Their actions were bitterly opposed by the citizens of neighbouring Penryn who rightly feared they would soon be overshadowed as a port. Falmouth's status as the most important port in Cornwall was confirmed when it became a Royal Mail packet station (to carry the mail overseas)

38. Arwenack House in Falmouth was the home of the piratical Killigrews.

in 1688. Its first sponsor, Sir John IV, is also remembered for a lengthy, acrimonious, and expensive divorce battle when his estranged wife fled from Arwenack and was given shelter by his opponents in Penryn.

In *The Survey of Cornwall* Richard Carew praised the location of Arwenack writing

> After the declining hill hath delivered you down from this castle [Pendennis], Arwenacke entertaineth you with a pleasing view, for the same standeth so far within the haven's mouth that it is protected from the sea storms, and yet so near thereunto as it yieldeth a ready passage out, ...[16]

Arwenack had three wings around an open courtyard with the fourth side (facing the water) enclosed by a wall with gatehouse[17]. The house was burned down during the siege of Pendennis in 1646 when it was the headquarters of the besieging roundhead army and never fully restored. It was last rebuilt in the 1980s and split into several private homes[18]. Visitors today can see the exterior of Arwenack next to Discovery Quay and the National Maritime Museum. In front of the building is a large granite obelisk erected in 1737 by Martin Lister Killigrew (1666-1745) as a memorial to his wife's family. Martin married the daughter of Sir Peter Killigrew II (1634-1705) and added Killigrew to his own surname in the failed hope of carrying on the family line. Sir Peter II (the son of Sir Peter I) proved the last in the male line of Killigrews of Arwenack. His son George died before him in 1687, killed in a Penryn tavern brawl (some sources say a duel) without leaving an heir. Martin Lister Killigrew and his wife had no children and Arwenack descended through another of Sir Peter II's daughters[19]. The obelisk was given no inscription by Martin Lister Killigrew so that its purpose was unclear to passers-by until the local history society added a plaque in 1987 telling the flamboyant story of the Killigrews of Arwenack.

Pendennis Castle and St Mawes Castle were held for the king in the early years of the Civil War (1642-1651). Falmouth was an important royalist port to bring in arms and supplies from abroad and a base to attack parliamentary shipping in the Channel. The first member of the royal family in flight to arrive at Pendennis Castle was Queen Henrietta Maria (1609-1669), wife of the beleaguered King Charles I, on her way to escape by sea to France in July 1644. The queen had left her husband's court in Oxford and parted from him three months before. Her great concern was to avoid capture by parliament when she could be used as a bargaining counter against the king. After a shaky start to their marriage husband and wife had formed a strong relationship; in her letters Henrietta Maria addresses Charles as 'My dear heart'.

The queen was heavily pregnant and suffering badly with arthritis or some other painful condition[20]. She was carried on a litter and her progress through the west country was slow. On 16 June in Exeter, Henrietta Maria gave birth to a daughter, her ninth and last child. Only two weeks after the birth, with the roundhead army closing in, the queen was forced to move on again leaving her tiny daughter behind in the care of a lady-in-waiting. The queen's motivation was clear from a letter Henrietta Maria wrote to her husband from Exeter

> I will show you by this last action that there is nothing that lies so near my heart as your safety. My life is but a small thing compared to that. For in the present state of affairs your condition would be in great peril if you came to my relief, and I know that your affection would make you risk all for my sake. And so I prefer to risk this miserable life of mine, a thing worthless enough in itself, saving so far as it is precious to you. My dear heart, farewell.[21]

When Henrietta Maria arrived at Pendennis her situation was still perilous. Parliament was aware of the queen's plan to escape to France and had ships at sea ready to intercept her. Henrietta Maria embarked from Falmouth on 14 July 1644 onboard a Dutch ship called the *George*. Her small fleet was pursued by parliament's ships that got close enough to fire shots and damage the rigging of the *George*. The queen remained defiant in the face of danger ordering the captain to destroy his ship rather than allow her to be captured. In the event the Dutch ships outdistanced their pursuers, and the queen reached the safety of the Brittany coast[22]. Henrietta Maria was a French princess by birth and was welcomed to the French court. She continued to plead the royalist cause in exile, but she would never see her husband again.

The second member of the royal family to escape through Pendennis, in March 1646, was Henrietta Maria's son Charles (1630-1685) the duke of Cornwall and future King Charles II. Fifteen-year-old Charles was commander in name of his father's army in the west country but had little say in the real decisions. The plan had been to fortify Pendennis as Charles's headquarters but by the time the prince arrived at the castle in February 1646 it was clear he must flee Cornwall. The roundhead army reached Launceston in north Cornwall on 25 February and was at Bodmin by 2 March (map 2).

Minette's story – Henrietta Anne Stuart (1644-1670)

The baby girl born to Queen Henrietta Maria in Exeter on 16 June 1644 in the turmoil of the Civil War was christened Henrietta after her mother. Later, when she joined her mother in exile in France, Anne was added as a second name in honour of Queen Anne of France. The little girl's brother Charles (the future Charles II) to whom she would become very close gave her the nickname of 'Minette'.

At two weeks old Minette was left behind in the care of her mother's friend and lady-in-waiting, Lady Anne Dalkeith. When Exeter surrendered to parliament in April 1646 Minette and her guardian were taken into custody and moved to Oatlands Palace in Surrey. Lady Dalkeith had been told by the king not to be separated from his daughter in any circumstances. She was horrified to discover that parliament intended to dismiss her and decided to escape and take Minette to her mother in France.

In July 1646 they slipped secretly away from Oatlands dressed in ragged clothes and with Minette disguised as a boy called Pierre. Lady Dalkeith walked all the way to Dover (some ninety miles) carrying Minette on her shoulders[23]. In the way of two-year-olds Minette indignantly announced to everyone they met that she was not a boy but a princess! At Dover they took ship to France where at the French court Minette was reunited with her mother.

Queen Henrietta Maria hoped Minette might marry her cousin King Louis XIV of France, but in the end she married his younger brother Philippe Duke of Orléans known at the French court as 'Monsieur'. The marriage was not a success. Monsieur was an effeminate bisexual who favoured his male lovers; Minette had affairs including with her brother-in-law Louis XIV who may have been the father of her first child.

Minette was taken ill with stomach pains and died aged only twenty-six. Poison was suspected but modern medicine suggests it was more likely natural causes, perhaps peritonitis (a bacterial infection). Minette has a place in British history as the founder of the Stuart line of claimants to our throne. The current Stuart claimant is Minette's eight times great-grandson, Franz Duke of Bavaria. To supporters he is King Franz of Great Britain and Ireland.

39. The young Charles Duke of Cornwall, the future King Charles II.

That same night Charles set sail for the Scilly Isles onboard a frigate called the *Phoenix*[24]. During the voyage he took the helm, and he discovered a life-long love of sailing and the sea[25]. From the Scilly Isles Charles moved to Jersey in the Channel Islands before in June 1646 he joined his mother in France.

On 15 March 1646 the royalist army surrendered to parliament at Tresillian Bridge near Truro. St Mawes Castle capitulated but the governor of Pendennis Castle, Sir John Arundell of Trerice, refused to hand over the castle. At seventy Sir John was an old man by the standards of the time but the doughty Cornishman stood firm.

Sir, the Castle was committed to my government by His Majesty, who by our laws hath the command of the Castles and Forts of this Kingdom, ... I wonder that you demand the Castle without authority from His Majesty, which if I should render, I brand myself and my posterity with the indelible character of Treason. And having taken less than two minutes resolution, I resolve that I will here bury myself before I deliver up this Castle to such as fight against His Majesty, and that nothing you can threaten is formidable to me in respect of the loss of loyalty and conscience.[26]

The siege of Pendennis lasted for five months. Inside the castle were eight hundred royalist troops with around two hundred women and children. The roundheads blockaded Pendennis by both land and sea, supplies soon ran low, and starvation threatened. Sir John wrote 'it is now come to the last with us' 'fedd upon bread and water'[27]. He negotiated honourable terms of surrender and on 17 August 1646 *Jack for the King* (as he became known) marched out of Pendennis at the head of his troops with trumpets sounding and all flags flying[28]. Sir John did not live to see the restoration of the monarchy, but his son Richard was created a baron by a grateful King Charles II. Richard had been with his father during the siege of Pendennis.

Visitors to Pendennis today enter the castle through an imposing gatehouse in the Elizabethan ramparts (that withstood the Civil War

40. Built with rising ground behind it, St Mawes Castle could not be defended in the Civil War.

siege) to emerge on a large parade ground where Henry VIII's castle at one end faces the Royal Garrison Artillery Barracks (built 1900-1902) at the other. Pendennis is particularly good fun to visit on days when there are live-action events themed on its illustrious history. *Pirate Attack* reflects its early days and re-enacts the garrison defending the Tudor castle against Spanish marauders. *Pendennis at War* presents the castle as in World War II. Pendennis last saw action and fired on German gunboats in the run up to D-Day in 1944. My favourite event is the *Grand Medieval Joust* when Pendennis is alive with medieval hustle and bustle and knights in armour mounted on their war horses thunder at each other down the parade ground. My small granddaughter was thrilled!

7.

RESTORMEL CASTLE AND PLACE HOUSE FOWEY

When Queen Victoria arrived at Restormel Castle on the morning of 8 September 1846 after an uncomfortable carriage drive from Fowey (see chapter 3) it was the first royal visit for centuries. Restormel was granted to the duchy of Cornwall on its creation in 1337 and five hundred years later belonged to Victoria's young son Bertie as the current duke. Restormel is strongly associated with the first duke of Cornwall. He was Edward of Woodstock (1330-1376) the eldest son of King Edward III who is better known in history as *the Black Prince*. Standing in the ruins of what were the royal apartments I could easily imagine the excitement when *the Black Prince* arrived with his knights to hold court at Restormel for the first time in August 1354. The curator told me many visitors feel this same sense of history. *The Black Prince* is fondly remembered in Cornwall as a good landlord who abated his rents during the catastrophic pandemic known as the *Black Death* (bubonic plague)[1]. The first deadly wave of the plague struck Cornwall in 1349 and wiped out around one third of the population[2]. After *the Black Prince*'s death, Restormel was largely neglected by the later dukes of Cornwall and fell into decay.

Restormel Castle occupies a commanding position above the river Fowey just north of Lostwithiel (map 6). It was built soon after the Norman Conquest to control a crossing point of the river. The castle was rebuilt as a royal residence in the late thirteenth century by Edmund Earl of Cornwall (1249-1300) the grandson of King John and cousin of King Edward I (see chart 3). Earl Edmund moved the centre of his earldom from Launceston Castle in north Cornwall to Lostwithiel to be closer to the tin mines that produced a major source of his income[3]. He built the complex of buildings in Lostwithiel known as the Duchy Palace for the administration of his earldom and remodelled Restormel Castle as his residence. When Earl Edmund died without heirs in 1300 Restormel reverted to the crown. In 1337 it was part of the extensive property granted to the new dukedom of Cornwall on its creation.

41. Restormel Castle at Lostwithiel where the first duke of Cornwall held his court. (Shutterstock/Paul Nash)

Earl Edmund rebuilt Restormel with an impressive circular stone Keep (or main building) housing the luxurious royal apartments. It was the custom then for great lords to travel constantly from castle to castle with a retinue of knights and ladies taking furniture, household goods, and servants with them. The Keep was only used when the lord was in residence. This is where *the Black Prince* held his court and received homage from his Cornish tenants in 1354. From the circular internal courtyard visitors can walk through the ruins of these apartments – the Great Hall, Lord's Chamber, Chapel, Lady's Chamber, and Guest Room.

When the lord was absent Restormel was managed on his behalf by a powerful local official called the steward. He lived and worked in the part of the castle called the Bailey. This was a large fenced-in compound adjacent to the Keep filled with more mundane buildings including offices, kitchens, storerooms, bakery, brewhouse, and stables. None of these buildings have survived the centuries but the Bailey still provides a service function for the castle. Nowadays it houses the ticket office, shop, and visitor toilets!

When *the Black Prince* came to stay at Restormel Castle in August 1354 he was already famous as the victor of the Battle of Crecy (26 August 1346) at the start of The Hundred Years War against France (1337-1453). The prince was only sixteen when he was given his first command at this battle by his father King Edward III. Crecy is where *the Black Prince* forged his military reputation. He lived before the art of portraiture and illustration 42, taken from an early twentieth century children's history book, is an imaginary picture[4].

The picture shows the prince picking up the helmet of blind King John of Bohemia after the English victory at Crecy. The blind king was a byword for valour internationally. He insisted on being led into the battle and died fighting for the French. The legend goes that to honour his memory *the Black Prince* adopted the dead king of Bohemia's badge of three ostrich feathers and motto of *Ich Dien* (I serve) for his own badge and motto as the prince of Wales. This title had been bestowed on him by his father King Edward III in 1343.

The nickname of *the Black Prince* did not arise in his lifetime and dates from the Tudor period. The derivation is unclear – possibly it was a reference to the colour of his armour; possibly a negative title given him by the French, whom he spent much of his career fighting against.

42. After his victory at Crecy *the Black Prince* picks up the helmet of blind King John of Bohemia, slain in the battle.

When *the Black Prince* returned to hold court at Restormel again at Christmas 1362 he was accompanied by his wife. In October 1361 he had married Princess Joan of Kent and she was the first duchess of Cornwall. An intriguing thing about the prince is that he did not marry until the late age (for those days) of thirty-one. His father, Edward III, had married at fifteen and was seventeen when his son was born. *The Black Prince's* choice of wife was also controversial. Joan was not (like his father's choice) a very young foreign princess selected for reasons of state, but a recently widowed cousin in her thirties with a tangled marital history and a bigamous marriage in her past.

Joan of Kent was the daughter of Edmund Earl of Kent, a younger son of King Edward I. She was called *the Fair Maid of Kent* and a contemporary historian described her as

... in her time the most beautiful woman in all the realm of England and the most loved ... [5]

Joan's father was executed on trumped up charges of treason when she was a toddler, and she was brought up in the royal household with *the Black Prince's* sisters. She and the prince must have known each other from childhood – perhaps a long-time love for Joan was the reason why he waited so long to marry. In 1341 when she was around thirteen (some of the dates are uncertain) Joan made a suitable dynastic marriage to William Montague, heir to the earldom of Salisbury. But some years later she claimed that this marriage was bigamous because she had previously been married in secret to a much lower ranking knight called Thomas Holand. There was little evidence of this pre-teen marriage, but Joan stuck to her story. Her marriage to William Montague was annulled by the Pope and she remarried Thomas Holand.

Historians have mostly accepted Joan's story. An alternative version of events however, is that Joan and Thomas Holand fell in love after she was married to William Montague and came up with the story of their earlier secret wedding to get her out of this unwanted relationship[6]. Whichever version you prefer, Joan and Thomas were married for eleven years and had five children together. Joan was her father's heiress and Thomas became earl of Kent in right of his wife. In October 1361, less than a year after Holand's death on active service in France, Joan married for the third time to *the Black Prince*.

Richard Earl of Cornwall and his castles

Richard of Cornwall (1209-1272) was the second son of King John and only a year younger than his brother King Henry III who succeeded their father in 1216 aged nine. In 1225, sixteen-year-old Richard was endowed with vast properties in Cornwall by his brother and soon after made earl of Cornwall. Richard's revenues from the lucrative Cornish tin mines helped to make him one of the richest princes in Europe.

Richard of Cornwall was not content to be the brother of a king and aspired to a throne of his own. He holds a unique position in history as the only Englishman to be elected as Holy Roman emperor, overlord of vast domains in Germany and across Europe. Cornish money bribed the German princes who voted for the emperor but when Richard was elected in 1256 it was by only a majority (4 out of 7 votes) with the minority electing their own candidate. Richard was defeated by the intricacies of German politics and, unable to impose his authority, he returned to England. This period in the history of the Holy Roman Empire is known as 'the Interregnum' and the two rival would-be emperors as 'the Little Kings'.

43. Launceston Castle was the headquarters of Richard Earl of Cornwall.

Richard made several visits to Cornwall where he extensively remodelled Launceston Castle as his headquarters. Launceston Castle, on the border with Devon (map 2), was built by Robert Count of Mortain, the half-brother of William the Conqueror, to control the northern entry into Cornwall over the river Tamar. Count Robert also built Trematon Castle near Saltash to control the southern entry. Launceston Castle towers over the town

44. Tintagel Castle was one of the four great castles of Richard Earl of Cornwall.

of the same name and is visible from miles around. I was nearly blown away climbing the steep flight of steps into the Keep. The curator has a wind machine and if the wind gets too strong, visitors are not allowed to go up.

Richard had a hobby of collecting Cornish castles and used his position as overlord to acquire these[7]. Launceston Castle was part of the property granted to him in 1225. In 1236 he swapped some lands for Tintagel Castle on the north coast of Cornwall; in 1268 he persuaded the heiress Ysolda de Cardinham to grant him Restormel Castle; and in 1270 he bought Trematon Castle from its previous owners. All four of his great castles would form part of the new duchy of Cornwall in 1337 and all are still owned by the duke of Cornwall today.

Richard of Cornwall married three times and left one surviving son. Earl Edmund (1249-1300) was the last earl of Cornwall to spend time in the county. He died without an heir in 1300 and Richard's line became extinct. The earldom of Cornwall went through two more brief creations. In 1307 Edward II gave the title to his crony Piers Gaveston (died 1312); in 1330 Edward III gave it to his younger brother John of Eltham (died 1336).

When King Edward III elevated Cornwall to a duchy in 1337 for his eldest son, he included the lands and castles of the old earldom of Richard of Cornwall.

The Black Prince's parents put a brave face on what was hardly the ideal royal marriage. Edward III appointed his son as ruler of the principality of Aquitaine that belonged to the English crown. The couple stayed at Restormel until spring 1363 and then sailed for France[8]. *The Black Prince* had so far met with success after success in France, winning the Battle of Crecy in 1346 and the Battle of Poitiers in 1356, when the king of France himself was captured. But Aquitaine was hard to govern and proved a step too far. *The Black Prince* and his wife were at the centre of a lavish court in Bordeaux. But his mission was a failure and he returned to England in 1371 a sick man, debilitated by repeated attacks of what was probably dysentery[9]. For the remaining years of his life the prince was an invalid; he died in 1376 at the age of forty-five. The following year, on the death of Edward III, his ten-year-old son with Joan became King Richard II.

45. The circular keep at Restormel was a luxurious royal residence.

Restormel is my favourite historic site to visit in Cornwall. The castle is not visible from the road and the best views are from a footpath across duchy of Cornwall land from the Duchy of Cornwall Garden Centre just over a mile away. The view of Restormel in the distance is very different than it would have been in the time of *the Black Prince* when the castle walls were rendered and whitewashed to stand out starkly in the surrounding deer park. In 1846, when Victoria visited, Restormel would have looked different again with the walls shrouded in ivy as a picturesque landscape ruin. The ivy was stripped off as a conservation measure when the government Ministry of Works took over the maintenance of Restormel in 1925. The duke of Cornwall at that time was the future King Edward VIII and, after his abdication, duke of Windsor. Restormel is now managed by English Heritage (successor to the Ministry of Works), but still owned by the duchy of Cornwall. The footpath from the Duchy of Cornwall Garden Centre skirts Restormel Manor (previously called Trinity House). This also belongs to the duchy of Cornwall and is where the current duke and duchess stay on visits to Cornwall.

From the car park at Restormel the footpath goes up through the fields on the hillside behind the castle to Leadenhill Wood and (what was when Victoria came) the Barngate level of the Restormel Iron Mine[10]. Small pieces of iron ore litter the side of the footpath and I brought one home as a souvenir. On top of the hill near Barngate Farm a danger sign next to the footpath warns of a mine shaft. So far as I can discover this was the entrance to the Restormel Iron Mine that Victoria and Albert went down after their visit to Restormel Castle on 8 September 1846.

Iron mining in Cornwall was never as economically significant as copper or tin mining for which Cornwall was a major world producer. The Gwennap copper mining area near Redruth was so productive it was called *the richest square mile on earth*! Albert had visited the surface at Gwennap the previous day while the royal yacht was moored at Falmouth. The visit to Restormel Iron Mine was organised by Richard Taylor, mineral agent for the duchy of Cornwall, who joined the royal entourage at Falmouth. In her journal Victoria thought 'Mr Taylor deserves the greatest credit for all the arrangements. He and his father are what are called Adventurers [proprietors] of the Mine.'[11]

Victoria's visit to the iron mine caused huge excitement and accounts by the miners appeared in the local newspaper. Writing in the *Royal Cornwall Gazette* the mine captain (head of mining operations) told how the queen's arrival was a surprise as they were expecting only her husband.

> I received a letter one evening ... to say how Prince Albert was coming to our main [mine] the next morning. In the morning, sure 'nuf, we see the chay [light carriage] coming and who should be in it but the Queen, so well as the Prence [prince]. The Queen got out of the chay and ran about in the wet grass like a Billy! [goat] Mr Taylor says to me 'Is it safe for the Queen to go in the main?'. 'Safe' says I 'Tes as safe as the rock of Gibraltar'. So the drams [trams or wagons] was broft forth and some straw throwed into one and some green baize after it and the Queen skipt in like a lamb – and I do believe that I touched her.[12]

The story was taken up by a miner who described how the queen and prince were pulled into the mine in the wagon down a sloping tunnel (called an adit) and how Albert hewed off a piece of iron ore at the mine face.

> ... the queen and Prince Albert went in the first Wagon ... with 4 [miners] pulling wagon by a rope ... Upwards of 200 fathoms then the Queen and Prince Albert walked 14 fathoms through the level. I put the Pick in Prince Albert's hands Wich he took it And broke a stone of ore. I Hold My Hat for him to break it in. He took it out of the Hat and Put it in his pocket. I am happy to let you know That we never make the least Shade of Blunder Whatever ...[13]

Illustration 46 is an artist's impression of Victoria at the mine workings[14]. When the royal couple emerged back into daylight from the tunnel 'One hundred and twenty miners were ready to cheer them as they drove off, all red, like injians [Indians] from the red ore of the main.'[15] Albert was presented with two miners' hats to take home and the queen ordered fifty sovereigns to be distributed among the miners. At a civic dinner to celebrate the event the proposer of the toast proudly declaimed

The hand that swings the sceptre of England did not feel denigrated by touching the rough iron wagon or inhaling the same air with the men.[16]

46. Victoria goes underground at the Restormel Iron Mine.

After their adventure at the iron mine Victoria and Albert returned by carriage to Fowey where they were shown around Place House before reboarding the royal yacht *Victoria and Albert* in Fowey harbour. Place House had been the home of the Treffry family for seven centuries since Thomas Treffry married the heiress of Place and Fowey. It is still privately owned by the family and not open to the public. Thomas's grandson John Treffry fought with *the Black Prince* in France and was knighted at the battle of Poitiers in 1356 for capturing the French royal standard[17]. His descendant, another Thomas Treffry, fortified the medieval house with battlements and a tower after the French raided Fowey in 1457. Thomas was away from home in the service of the king (Henry VI) and in a famous family story, Place was resolutely defended by his wife Elizabeth who poured boiling lead down on the French attackers and fought them off[18]. Their three sons John, William, and Thomas supported the Lancastrian cause during the Wars of the Roses and prospered after Henry VII took the throne. Place House was remodelled in the Tudor style. Thomas's son Thomas (who inherited Place) supervised the building of two of Henry VIII's coastal defence castles – St Mawes Castle (chapter 6) and St Catherine's Castle at the entrance to Fowey harbour (map 6).

When Richard Carew wrote *The Survey of Cornwall*, he praised Place as a 'fair and ancient house, castle-wise builded [fortified] and ... overlooketh the town and haven with a pleasant prospect.'[19]. Situated in the maze of small streets in Fowey, the house is hidden from the outside world. The best view is from across the water on the other side of Fowey harbour. My husband and I took the ferry to Bodinnick (map 6) to find the ancient waterside promenade called Hall Walk. Richard Carew called Hall Walk 'a place of diversified pleasings' and thought everyone would like it as much as he did if they went there[20]. King Charles I (1600-1649) was walking along Hall Walk on 17 August 1644 (during the Civil War) when he narrowly avoided death from a shot fired by the parliamentary troops in Fowey. A commemorative plaque on the spot records that a poor fisherman was killed standing where

47. The view of Fowey from Hall Walk
with Place House to the right of the church.

the king had been moments before. The views of Fowey from Hall
Walk are amazing with the crenelated walls and tall tower of Place
House clearly visible to the right of the church.

Illustration 48 from *The Illustrated London News* coverage of the
royal visit to Cornwall shows the royal carriage with Victoria and Albert
arriving at Place House. Victoria's host was the wealthy industrialist
Joseph Thomas Treffry (1782-1850), sometimes called *The King of Mid
Cornwall* for his importance to the local economy[21]. Joseph Thomas was
unusual in his day and age as an aristocrat who achieved great success
in business. His mines and quarries employed hundreds of Cornish
workers and his legacy includes the magnificent viaduct spanning
the Luxulyan valley near Lostwithiel (built to transport water and
materials to his mines) and the harbour at Par near Fowey (built to
ship out the extracted ore).

48. The carriage with Victoria and Albert drives up to Place House in Fowey.

Joseph Thomas Treffry was born Joseph Thomas Austen and changed his surname to Treffry later in life. His mother Susanna Austen (1748-1842) was a Treffry by birth and inherited Place from her brother in 1779[22]. In the eighteenth century the Treffry family ran short of sons and the succession to Place passed three times through the female line. Chart 9 shows extracts from the Treffry family tree.

Susanna Austen was widowed young and moved to Place with her son when Joseph Thomas was four years old[23]. The Treffry family ancestral home had fallen into poor repair and Joseph Thomas would spend much of his adult life using his great wealth to rebuild it. He seems to have acted as his own architect and chose the romantic mock-gothic architectural style that was so fashionable in the first half of the nineteenth century. The project took more than thirty years and cost an enormous one hundred and twenty thousand pounds[24]. It is difficult to precisely state the equivalent in money terms today, but it could be in the region of fifteen million pounds[25].

The last room to be completed was the Porphyry Hall using stone entirely from Joseph Thomas's own quarries (porphyry rock is similar to granite). 'The old Gentleman showed us all over the house,' Victoria wrote in her journal '& into an unfinished Porphyry Hall, the stone & porphyry of which all comes from Cornwall.'[26]. Joseph Thomas was proud of the queen's reaction to the crowning achievement of his restoration.

We went into the Porphyry Hall and on entering which Her Majesty made a full stop opposite the great arch and exclaimed: 'That is magnificent.'[27]

He must have seen the royal visit as the pinnacle of his career. *The King of Mid Cornwall* delivered a loyal address to the queen from the citizens of Fowey and presented Prince Albert with 'a splendid drawing of Place House' and 'a beautiful model of Restormel Castle, made of Cork' 'which the Prince was most graciously pleased to accept.'[28] Two slabs of porphyry were sent on afterwards to Osborne House[29].

Place House was the last engagement of the royal visit to Cornwall in 1846. Victoria and Albert walked back to the royal yacht through the narrow streets of Fowey. In the afternoon the royal flotilla set off for the Isle of Wight where the royal family arrived home at Osborne House at nine o'clock the next morning.

8.

RETURN TO OSBORNE HOUSE

On the morning of Wednesday, 9 September 1846 the royal yacht arrived back at Osborne on the Isle of Wight at the end of Queen Victoria's royal visit to Cornwall. On board were the queen, her husband Prince Albert, and their two eldest children. Victoria was sorry their cruise had come to an end: 'The life of independence one leads on board, — & the pure air one gets in such quantity on deck, is so delightful.'[1] But she was also pleased to be back at Osborne and reunited with her three younger children left behind in the nursery. 'Drove up at once to Osborne [House], where we found our 3 little people very flourishing. — Alice [three], very rosy, & Helena [three months] sitting up'. The third 'little people' was two-year-old Affie, short for Alfred.

Victoria and Albert bought the Osborne estate in 1845 as a country retreat away from the hurly-burly of official life in London. The royal family were temporarily living in the existing house on the site while a new Osborne House was being built by Albert. 'After luncheon' Victoria wrote in her journal for the day of their return from Cornwall 'we went over our new house, which is really lovely, & fast getting furnished. The Nurseries are ready & our rooms, which are beautiful, nearly so.'

A few days later, on 14 September 1846, the family moved in and slept for the first time in their new home. Victoria's maid of honour Miss Lucy Kerr (who had accompanied them on the visit to Cornwall) hurled an old shoe after Victoria as she crossed the threshold. Miss Kerr was from Scotland, and this was an old Scottish tradition to bring good luck[2]. At dinner that evening the company drank a housewarming toast and Albert spoke a simple prayer in German to bless the new house.

> Gott behüte dieses Haus
> Und die da gehen ein und aus[3]
> [God protect this house
> And our coming in and going out]

Lady Sarah Lyttelton in charge of the royal nursery was relieved that it had all gone well and 'Nobody caught cold or smelt paint...'[4].

When Victoria and Albert were first married, their main royal residences were Buckingham Palace in London, Windsor Castle a few miles to the west, and the Royal Pavilion in Brighton. These official residences were out of date, inconvenient, insanitary, badly run, and totally unsuitable for a young family. One of Albert's early tasks was to reorganise the running of the royal palaces, bringing this under tighter control and rooting out waste, pilfering, corruption, and mismanagement. Privacy and security were also issues. At Windsor Castle the public had access to the grounds; at Brighton the queen was mobbed every time she set foot outside the Pavilion door! When Victoria was lying-in (recovering) after the birth of Vicky at Buckingham Palace, her midwife Mrs Lilly found a boy who had infiltrated the queen's rooms and was hiding under the sofa! Victoria and Albert wanted a real home of their own in the countryside where they could enjoy some privacy. Victoria had happy memories of the Isle of Wight from visiting with her mother as a child and the acquisition of the royal steam yacht *Victoria and Albert* in 1843 brought the island within comfortable travelling reach.

49. Osborne House with the royal family's private wing
called the Pavilion on the right.

Albert built the new Osborne House to his own design in the style
of an Italian villa with sweeping grounds and views down to the Solent
(the strip of water between the Isle of Wight and Portsmouth on the
mainland). The prince had a free hand since Osborne was the royal
family's private property bought with their own money, and never an
official royal palace.

As Victoria put it, the project was free '... from all Woods and
Forests, and other charming departments who really are the plague
of one's life.'[5] ('Woods and Forests' were the government department
responsible for building work and repairs on royal palaces[6].) Albert
flouted convention and chose not to appoint an architect, working
directly with the builder Thomas Cubitt. It was a happy collaboration.
The new house was equipped with all the latest building technology
including cast-iron (instead of wooden) beams, insulated walls and
floors (insulated with seashells) and indoor plumbing with running hot
water, flush toilets, and showers!

The design achieved everything Albert hoped for with a private wing for the royal family called the Pavilion. This was connected by the Grand Corridor to the Main Wing with audience rooms and a council chamber for conducting state business and the Household Wing with accommodation for courtiers. The Main Wing also had suites of guest rooms and one for Victoria's mother the duchess of Kent. Despite their earlier estrangement Victoria was now reconciled to her mother by the good offices of Albert. Albert was fond of the duchess who was his aunt (his father's sister). Building work continued at Osborne into the 1850s and the final wing with a vast ballroom called the Durbar Room was not completed until long after Albert's death.

In her journal for their first day in the new house Victoria enthusiastically described the family's accommodation in the Pavilion with receptions rooms on the ground floor (dining room, drawing room and billiard room), a suite for herself and Albert on the first floor (bedroom, sitting room, two dressing rooms and bathroom), and the nurseries and children's quarters on the second floor.

> All is so convenient, spacious & well carried out. Mr Cubitt has done it admirably. He is such an honest, kind good man. It appears to me like a dream to be here now in our own house, of [which] we laid the 1st stone only 15 months ago![7]

Osborne House was filled with works of art selected by Albert, including the serpentine items bought on the royal visit to Cornwall. Above the sideboard in the dining room the prince hung a copy of the famous group portrait of his young family in 1846 by the royal portrait artist Franz Xaver Winterhalter. This magnificent picture (see illustration 50) shows Victoria and Albert with their five eldest children – the two boys (Bertie and Affie) on the left next to Victoria, and the three girls (Vicky, Alice, and baby Helena) on the right. In 1862, just months after her father's death, Alice would be married in front of this picture in the dining room at Osborne. Her mother described the

50. The dining room with magnificent group portrait of Victoria and Albert and their five children in 1846.

scaled back and joyless ceremony as 'more a funeral than a wedding'[8]. Victoria herself would lay in state in the dining room at Osborne in January 1901.

At Osborne 'The whole Royal family, children, Queen and all seem to be out the whole day long'[9]. The children loved digging in the sand and searching for shells on the private beach and learned to swim in a collapsible swimming pool moored in the sea off the beach. Designed by Albert, this had a wooden grating floor that could be lowered or raised to suit the height of the child[10]. Even Victoria took a dip in the privacy of a horse-drawn bathing machine pulled into the sea. 'I thought it delightful' she wrote 'til I put my head under the water, when I thought I should be stifled.'[11]

Albert wanted to give his own children the same happy experience he remembered from childhood summers with his brother Ernst at Schloss Rosenau in Coburg where he was born. He created a special children's garden at Osborne where each child had a small plot of earth and learned to cultivate fruit, flowers, and vegetables using miniature garden tools and wheelbarrows. Albert would pay market price to the child for any produce successfully grown[12].

In 1854 a furnished playhouse called the Swiss Cottage was added to the children's garden. This was a scaled down version of a Swiss chalet based on the one in the garden at Schloss Rosenau[13]. Here the children were taught the rudiments of good housekeeping. The Swiss Cottage had a miniature shop called 'Spratt Grocer to Her Majesty' to learn the price of goods[14] and how to keep household accounts[15]; a kitchen with a range for cooking; and a dining room upstairs where the children could entertain their parents to lunch or tea. The fun and playacting were all part of Albert's educational scheme. Four more children were born before the family was complete – Louise in 1848, Arthur in 1850, Leopold in 1853, and Beatrice in 1857.

51. Queen Victoria's sitting room at Osborne with twin desks where she and Albert worked side by side – Victoria on the left desk, Albert on the right.

Osborne after Queen Victoria

By great good fortune Queen Victoria's rooms in Osborne House have been preserved in time as she left them. No one else ever lived in these rooms. After Victoria's death in 1901 the new King Edward VII had no use for Osborne as a private home. He already had a country house at Sandringham in Norfolk. On his coronation day in August 1902 the king gave Osborne to the nation. The Main and Household Wings were converted for use as a convalescence home for officers and a royal naval college was built in the grounds to train boy cadets. Both the future kings Edward VIII and George VI attended this as boys. But by the king's wish the Pavilion Wing was left untouched as a memorial to his mother.

In 1904 some rooms on the ground floor of the Pavilion were opened to the public as a museum. Victoria and Albert's suite of rooms on the first floor however were sealed behind locked iron gates to prevent any unauthorised access. The bedroom where Victoria died became a shrine where members of the royal family came to remember her. Otherwise for fifty years only the house governor and the cleaners went through the gates to maintain the rooms. In 1954 Queen Elizabeth II gave permission for the gates to be unlocked and Queen Victoria's rooms were opened to the public.

Osborne House is a magical place to visit. The desks where Victoria and Albert worked side by side are still in their private sitting room covered with family photos and mementoes. You get a real feeling at Osborne for how Victoria and Albert lived and their happy family life before his death took the joy away for Victoria. Osborne is an English Heritage property. I think the best time to go is in the spring when the primroses are out.

Osborne became a very special place for Victoria. In Albert's lifetime they both usually celebrated their birthdays here – Victoria's in May and Albert's in August. The day of Victoria's birthday would begin early with a band playing on the terrace below her bedroom and bunches of flowers from her children[16]. Albert's birthday was always celebrated with a rural fete like the one that took place in the middle of the royal visit to Cornwall in 1846 (see chapter 3). After Albert's early death in December 1861 at the age of forty-two it was to Osborne that Victoria retreated to nurse her grief. And it was at Osborne that Victoria herself died, nearly forty years later, in January 1901. Victoria expressed the peaceful feeling she found at Osborne in a letter to her eldest daughter Vicky.

> Osborne is really too lovely. ... that peaceful enjoyment that one has here of dear Osborne – the deep blue sea, myriads of brilliant flowers – the perfume of orange-blossom, magnolias, honeysuckles – roses etc. of all descriptions on the terrace, the quiet and retirement all make it a perfect paradise – which I always deeply grieve to leave.[17]

To find out more about the fascinating life of Queen Victoria and her family see my series of books on *The Colourful Personal Life of Queen Victoria*. Further details are on page 168.

9.

THE DUCHY OF CORNWALL AND ITS ROYAL DUKES

In 1337, King Edward III created his seven-year-old eldest son the duke of Cornwall. At that time, it was the custom to refer to royal princes by the place where they were born, and the little boy was known as Edward of Woodstock. Edward grew up to be a famous soldier celebrated as the model of medieval chivalry. He is known in history as *the Black Prince*. He was duke of Cornwall for thirty-nine years but died the year before his father and never became king. Cornwall was the first English dukedom (or duchy) to be created and is the oldest and most senior of all the British dukedoms. For nearly seven hundred years, since *the Black Prince*, the duchy of Cornwall has been held by the eldest son of the reigning monarch. At the time of writing the current duke of Cornwall, and the longest serving (seventy years), is Prince Charles.

Duke of Cornwall is one of several titles held by the eldest son of the sovereign. Edward III also created his young son earl of Chester in 1333 and prince of Wales in 1343. The senior of these titles is that of prince of Wales first bestowed on the grandfather of *the Black Prince* in 1301. The title of duke of Cornwall is also important and (unlike that of prince of Wales) it passes as of right to the holder and does not have to be bestowed. Queen Victoria's son Bertie became the twenty-first duke of Cornwall on his birth in November 1841 since he was born the eldest son of the reigning monarch. The title of prince of Wales was bestowed on him a month later. Prince Charles automatically became twenty-fourth duke of Cornwall in February 1952, aged three, when his mother succeeded to the throne as Queen Elizabeth II. Charles was created prince of Wales some years later (in 1958) and publicly invested with that title as an adult, in a ceremony at Caernarvon Castle in 1969.

The story of the dukes of Cornwall is a thrilling panoply of royal history. The list of dukes is by no means identical to the rollcall of England's kings. In addition to well-known kings like Henry VIII and Charles II (the ninth and sixteenth dukes of Cornwall respectively), the list includes tragic princes such as Edward of Westminster (the fifth duke), who was the Lancastrian heir to the throne during the Wars of the Roses and killed at the battle of Tewkesbury in 1471, aged seventeen; forgotten princes like Arthur Tudor (the eighth duke), who was the first husband of Catherine of Aragon, but died at fifteen and was written out of history in favour of her second husband (his younger brother Henry VIII); and thwarted lives such as that of James Francis Edward Stuart (the seventeenth duke), known as *the Old Pretender*, who was exiled as a baby and never regained the crown lost by his father, James II.

Dukes of Cornwall feature in some of the most fascinating 'What ifs' in British history. If Henry VIII and Catherine of Aragon's baby son (the tenth duke) had not died as an infant but lived to adulthood there might never have been an English Reformation. If the thirteenth duke Henry Frederick Stuart (eldest son of James I) had not died of typhoid fever at eighteen there might not have been an English Civil War. Henry Frederick was a youth of great promise and would likely have made a better king than his disastrous younger brother Charles I (the fourteenth duke).

List of the royal dukes of Cornwall (with their dates as duke)
See chart 4 for more information

1. *Edward of Woodstock (the Black Prince) 1337-1376*
2. *Richard of Bordeaux, later King Richard II 1376-1377*
3. *Henry of Monmouth, later King Henry V 1399-1413*
4. *Henry of the house of Lancaster, later Henry VI 1421-1422*
5. *Edward of Westminster 1453-1471*
6. *Edward of the Sanctuary, briefly King Edward V 1471-1483*
7. *Edward of Middleham 1483-1484*
8. *Arthur Tudor 1486-1502*
9. *Henry Tudor, later King Henry VIII 1502-1509*
10. *Henry infant son of Henry VIII 1511*
11. *Henry second infant son of Henry VIII 1514*
12. *Edward Tudor, later King Edward VI 1537-1547*
13. *Henry Frederick Stuart 1603-1612*
14. *Charles Stuart, later King Charles I 1612-1625*
15. *Charles infant son of Charles I 1629*
16. *Charles Stuart, later Charles II 1630-1649*
17. *James Francis Edward Stuart (the Old Pretender) 1688*
18. *George Augustus, later King George II 1714-1727*
19. *Frederick Lewis 1727-1751*
20. *George, later King George IV 1762-1820*
21. *Albert Edward (Bertie), later King Edward VII 1841-1901*
22. *George, later King George V 1901-1910*
23. *Edward, later King Edward VIII and duke of Windsor 1910-1936*
24. *Charles 1952 to date*

Another reason the title of duke of Cornwall is important is because (again unlike the title of prince of Wales) the duchy of Cornwall is a private estate which provides the duke with a large income, currently running at more than £20 million a year. It is the duchy of Cornwall that makes Prince Charles a very rich man.

52. Trematon Castle near Saltash has been owned by the duke of Cornwall since the duchy was created in 1337.

When Edward III created the duchy under a charter of 1337, he endowed it with the vast landed estate of the old earldom of Cornwall that had reverted to the crown a few months before. This huge endowment was designed to provide an income for the heir to the throne independent of the crown. By the terms of the charter, the royal dukes of Cornwall are entitled to the income from the duchy but not to the capital assets that are held in trust for future dukes.

The endowment by Edward III included assets still owned by the duchy of Cornwall today. The four great castles of Richard of Cornwall (see chapter 7) belong to Prince Charles as the duke of Cornwall. Restormel, Launceston, and Tintagel are open to the public under the management of English Heritage; Trematon is leased to a private tenant who lives in a large Georgian house built in the grounds. Prince Charles owns the coastal foreshore (coastline) around Cornwall and the riverbeds of Cornish rivers. The endowment also included lands in other counties. One of the most profitable properties proved to be the rural manor of Kennington in Surrey where *the Black Prince* built his palace. This is now part of the London borough of Lambeth and home to *The Oval* cricket ground. The largest individual landholding of the duchy is some twenty-seven thousand hectares (sixty-seven thousand acres) of Dartmoor National Park in Devon. It is important to stress that the duchy of Cornwall has never owned the whole of the county of Cornwall. The duchy currently owns nearly fifty-three thousand hectares of land in total (one hundred and thirty thousand acres) and has property in twenty counties of England and Wales.

In addition to real property, the duchy of Cornwall was granted numerous rights and privileges previously reserved to the crown. The most valuable of these was the right to coinage (or the tax on tin) in the stannaries (tin mining areas). This was a lucrative source of income for the duke of Cornwall for centuries. Cornwall was a major world producer of smelted tin and it all had to pass through the duke's coinage halls to be quality checked and weighed and the coinage tax paid. The right to coinage was given up in return for an annuity only in 1838. The duchy today still holds arcane rights that might be considered inappropriate in the modern day. If you live in Cornwall and die intestate (without leaving a will and with no known relatives) your estate goes to Prince Charles as the duke of Cornwall. Another area of debate is the lack of application of taxation rules to the duchy. Prince Charles pays tax on a voluntary basis, but the question remains as to why the duchy of Cornwall should be exempt and what would be the right amount of tax if the same rules applied as to other entities.

Chart 4 gives brief details of the twenty-four dukes of Cornwall from *the Black Prince* to Prince Charles. It is difficult to be precise about the number of dukes as in theory a baby born the eldest son of the sovereign still holds the title even if he lives only briefly. The list of twenty-four includes two sons of Henry VIII and one of Charles I who died soon after birth. In earlier centuries infant deaths are not always well documented and the existence of a second baby son of Henry VIII and Catherine of Aragon is mentioned in some but not all sources.

Most dukes of Cornwall have, like Victoria's son Bertie (the twenty-first duke), come into the title at birth (eleven) or during childhood (a further nine). During Bertie's childhood the duchy was managed on his behalf by Prince Albert. Victoria gave her husband a free hand in the duchy and (in April 1842) appointed him as Lord Warden of the Stanneries[1]. This is the lead position on a body called the Prince's Council first set up by *the Black Prince* when the duchy was created. The Council and the position of Lord Warden still exist. It has a purely advisory role and executive powers rest with Prince Charles as duke.

With his customary thoroughness and diligence, Albert set about reforming the administration of the duchy of Cornwall and increasing the revenues. He was advised by the royal family mentor Baron Stockmar who suggested he

> ... avoid going too deep into details, which will only bewilder you. The fundamental principle to which you have to hold fast is that the Duchy is altogether a private affair with which neither the Government not its ministers have, or ought to have, anything to do.[2]

Under Albert's tenure the net revenues of the duchy quadrupled – from £11,536 in 1838 (not long before Albert took over) to £46,676 in 1861 (the year he died)[3]. The surplus accumulated during his childhood enabled Bertie to buy Sandringham House in Norfolk as his country estate when he reached the age of twenty-one[4]. Albert's failure, presumably caused by lack of faith in his son's ability, was to refuse to allow Bertie any involvement in duchy affairs during his lifetime.

Bertie's trip to Cornwall with his parents in 1846 was the first time a duke of Cornwall had visited Cornwall for two hundred years. The twenty princes who preceded him as duke of Cornwall showed little interest in spending time in the county that provided much of their income. Only two are known to have been in Cornwall – *the Black Prince* who twice made the arduous journey to hold his court in

53. The duke and duchess of Cornwall (Bertie and his wife Princess Alexandra
of Denmark) visit St Michael's Mount in 1865
(from *The Illustrated London News*).

Cornwall (see Restormel Castle in chapter 7) and the future Charles II
who was sent by his father as a teenager on campaign in the English
Civil War (see Pendennis Castle in chapter 6). The renowned Cornish
historian A.L. Rowse thought the royal connection through the duchy
of Cornwall had been a drain on the county rather than an advantage as
the royal dukes took the resources out of Cornwall to spend the money
elsewhere[5]. The exception may have been the first duke (*the Black
Prince*) who is reputed to have been a good landlord. A contemporary
wrote of him.

> Where the Lords of this world usually oppress and afflict their
> tenants and landholders, this lord always cared for his tenants,
> comforting them in many ways.[6]

Bertie and the three dukes who have followed him all visited Cornwall and took a closer interest in their Cornish property and tenants.

The five longest serving sovereigns and dukes of Cornwall

	Reign dates	Reign years	Dukedom dates	Dukedom years
Sovereigns				
Elizabeth II	1952 to date	70	–	–
Victoria	1837-1901	63	–	–
George III	1760-1820	59	–	–
James VI/I	1567-1625*	57	–	–
Henry III	1216-1272	56	–	–
Dukes of Cornwall				
Prince Charles	Current heir	–	1952 to date	70
Edward VII	1901-1910	9	1841-1901	59
George IV	1820-1830	10	1762-1820	57
The Black Prince	–	–	1337-1376	39
Edward VIII	1936	1	1910-1936	26

*1567 Scotland; 1603 England.

The list above shows the five longest-serving dukes of Cornwall. Together they held the duchy for over two hundred and fifty years but reigned as king for only twenty. *The Black Prince* was duke for thirty-nine years but died before his father and never became king. In total eleven of the twenty-four dukes of Cornwall did not live to succeed to the throne. Frederick Lewis (the nineteenth duke) held the duchy of Cornwall for twenty-three years but died unexpectedly at the age of forty-four. He was on very bad terms with his father George II and is known in history as *Poor Fred*. Several dukes of Cornwall who did come to the throne only had short reigns as king. Edward VIII (the twenty-third duke of Cornwall and fifth longest serving) followed his father as king in 1936 but abdicated less than a year later to marry Mrs Simpson and take the title duke of Windsor. The boy king Edward of the Sanctuary (the sixth duke) succeeded his father as Edward V in 1483 only to be deposed by his uncle Richard III two months later.

The list also shows that none of the five longest-serving British sovereigns were ever duke of Cornwall. Daughters are not eligible for the dukedom of Cornwall (surely something that needs to change) and Queen Elizabeth II (the longest-serving sovereign at seventy years and counting) did not have the title as heir while her father George VI was on the throne. He was not duke of Cornwall either because he was a second son and succeeded his brother Edward VIII. Even if females had been eligible for the duchy, Queen Victoria (the second longest-serving sovereign at sixty-three years) could not have been duke of Cornwall because she was heiress to her uncle William IV (and not to her father). George III (fifty-nine years) was the grandson (rather than the son) of his predecessor George II; James I (fifty-seven years) succeeded his cousin Elizabeth I; and Henry III (fifty-six years) reigned before the duchy of Cornwall was created.

There have been long periods in history when the duchy of Cornwall had no duke. This was because (like Henry VIII for much of his reign) the monarch did not have a son. The list of dukes in chart 4 also shows the periods since the creation of the duchy in 1337 when there was no duke of Cornwall in existence. During the sixteenth century, across the reigns of Henry VIII, Edward VI (died unmarried), Mary I (married but childless), and Elizabeth I (unmarried), there was a duke of Cornwall for only nineteen years and the duchy was vacant for eighty-one. In case of such a vacancy the duchy of Cornwall and its revenues revert temporarily to the sovereign. The terms of the charter still apply and the duchy vests automatically in the next duke of Cornwall as soon as he comes into existence. In the 1590s, towards the end of her reign, Queen Elizabeth I contravened the terms of the charter by selling off duchy lands to ease a cash shortage. This was subsequently held to be illegal when her successor (James I) came to the throne and the properties were recovered. On Elizabeth's death in 1603 the duchy had a duke for the first time in more than half a century. This was Prince Henry Frederick, the eldest son of James I.

There have been far fewer duchesses of Cornwall than there have been dukes – only ten duchesses to date as compared to twenty-four dukes. In the early centuries of the duchy's history many dukes died as children or waited until they came to the throne to marry. Before 1714 (when the duke of Hannover succeeded to the British throne as George I) there were seventeen dukes of Cornwall and only three duchesses.

List of the duchesses of Cornwall

1. *Joan of Kent wife of Edward of Woodstock (duke number 1)*
2. *Anne Neville wife of Edward of Westminster (number 5)*
3. *Catherine of Aragon wife of Arthur Tudor (number 8)*
4. *Caroline of Ansbach wife of George Augustus (number 18)*
5. *Augusta of Saxe-Gotha-Altenburg wife of Frederick Lewis (number 19)*
6. *Caroline of Brunswick wife of George IV (number 20)*
7. *Alexandra of Denmark wife of Edward VII (number 21)*
8. *Mary of Teck wife of George V (number 22)*
9. *Diana Spencer first wife of Prince Charles (number 24)*
10. *Camilla Parker-Bowles second wife of Prince Charles (number 24)*

The stories of the duchesses of Cornwall are as riveting as those of their dukes. Joan of Kent was a twice married widow with a scandalous past when she married *the Black Prince* and became the first duchess of Cornwall in 1361 (see chapter 7 for more on her story). Anne Neville was the daughter of the earl known as *Warwick the Kingmaker* for his role in switching sides to make and unmake kings during the Wars of the Roses (1455-1487). Anne was married in turn to husbands from opposing sides in this conflict (the houses of Lancaster and of York). She became duchess of Cornwall in 1470 on her marriage to Edward of Westminster (the fifth duke of Cornwall). He was the son of King Henry VI and the Lancastrian heir to the throne. After Edward's violent death the following year at the Battle of Tewkesbury, aged only seventeen, Anne married as her second husband the future King Richard III from the House of York. Catherine of Aragon is famous as the divorced wife of King Henry VIII. Catherine was duchess of Cornwall through her first marriage in 1501 to Henry's older brother Arthur Tudor (the eighth duke of Cornwall). The lengthy debate over whether her brief marriage to Arthur was consummated was a cause of the English Reformation.

54. The beautiful Princess Alexandra of Denmark became the seventh duchess of Cornwall when she married Bertie in 1863.

Since George I and the Hanoverians all the dukes of Cornwall have been married with one exception. Edward VIII married Wallis Simpson after his abdication as king and was a bachelor when he held the duchy. Bertie's duchess was the beautiful and popular Princess Alexandra of Denmark (the seventh duchess). Illustration 53 shows them visiting St Michael's Mount not long after their wedding in 1863. The story of Prince Charles's two marriages has tended to polarise opinion between supporters of his two duchesses – his first wife, Lady Diana Spencer (the ninth duchess), and his second, Camilla Parker-Bowles (the tenth).

The next duke and duchess of Cornwall, when Prince Charles becomes king, will be Prince William and his wife Catherine.

SKETCH MAPS

1. Queen Victoria's cruise to Cornwall and the Channel Islands
2. The county of Cornwall
3. Mount Edgcumbe and the River Tamar
4. St Michael's Mount and The Lizard
5. Pendennis Castle Falmouth and the River Fal
6. Fowey and Restormel Castle

1. QUEEN VICTORIA'S CRUISE TO CORNWALL
AND THE CHANNEL ISLANDS

First week of cruise
18-24 August 1846

Second week of cruise
2-9 September 1846

2. THE COUNTY OF CORNWALL

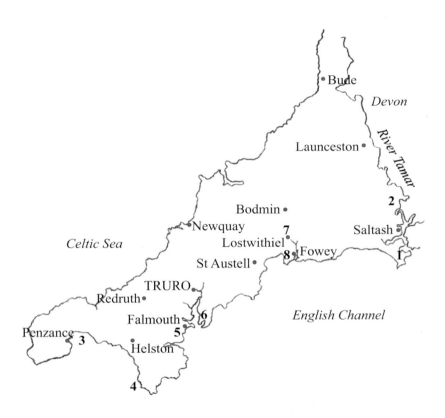

1. Mount Edgcumbe
2. Cotehele
3. St Michael's Mount
4. Kynance Cove
5. Pendennis Castle
6. St Mawes Castle
7. Restormel Castle
8. Place House Fowey

3. MOUNT EDGCUMBE AND THE RIVER TAMAR

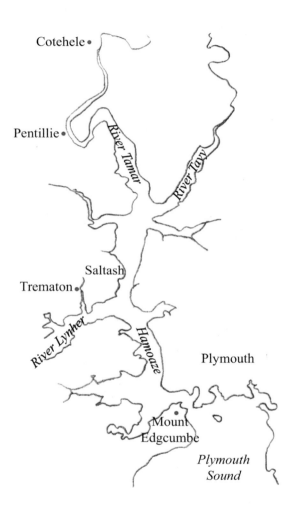

4. ST MICHAEL'S MOUNT AND THE LIZARD

5. PENDENNIS CASTLE FALMOUTH AND THE RIVER FAL

TRURO

Sunny Corner

Truro River

Tregothnan

River Fal

Trelissick

King Harry Ferry

Carclew

Carrick Roads

St Just in Roseland

Penryn

Trefusis

FALMOUTH

Arwenack

St Mawes Castle

Pendennis Castle

Swanpool

Falmouth Bay

St Anthony Head

6. FOWEY AND RESTORMEL CASTLE

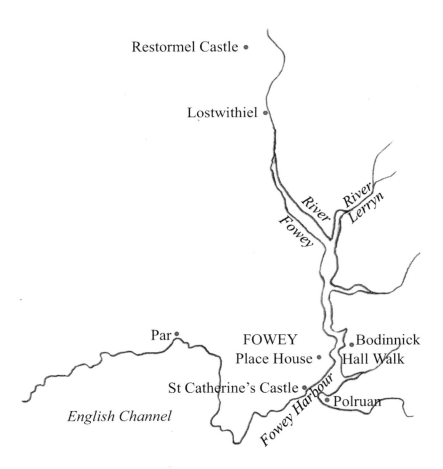

CHARTS AND FAMILY TREES

1. The family of Queen Victoria
2. How Queen Victoria succeeded to the British throne
3. From Richard of Cornwall to The Black Prince
   – the royal earls and dukes of Cornwall
4. The twenty-four royal dukes of Cornwall
5. The Edgcumbes at Cotehele and Mount Edgcumbe
6. The Mount Edgcumbe Succession
7. The St Aubyns at St Michael's Mount
8. The Killigrews of Arwenack Falmouth
9. The Treffrys of Place House Fowey

1. THE FAMILY OF QUEEN VICTORIA

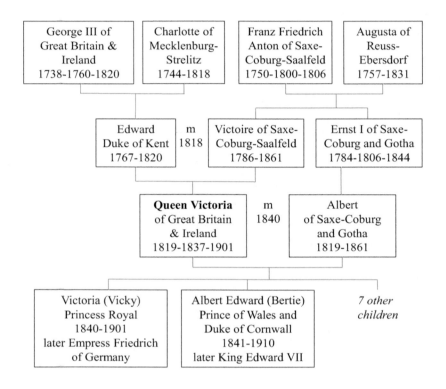

| George III of Great Britain & Ireland 1738-1760-1820 | Charlotte of Mecklenburg-Strelitz 1744-1818 | Franz Friedrich Anton of Saxe-Coburg-Saalfeld 1750-1800-1806 | Augusta of Reuss-Ebersdorf 1757-1831 |

Edward Duke of Kent 1767-1820 — m 1818 — Victoire of Saxe-Coburg-Saalfeld 1786-1861 — Ernst I of Saxe-Coburg and Gotha 1784-1806-1844

Queen Victoria of Great Britain & Ireland 1819-1837-1901 — m 1840 — Albert of Saxe-Coburg and Gotha 1819-1861

Victoria (Vicky) Princess Royal 1840-1901 later Empress Friedrich of Germany — Albert Edward (Bertie) Prince of Wales and Duke of Cornwall 1841-1910 later King Edward VII — *7 other children*

Chart shows the family of Queen Victoria beginning with her grandparents, two of whom she shared with her husband Prince Albert (who was also her first cousin). Not all family members are included.

Chart also shows the two children of Victoria and Albert who accompanied their parents on the visit to Cornwall in 1846. Their seven younger children are not shown in detail.

2. HOW QUEEN VICTORIA SUCCEEDED TO THE BRITISH THRONE

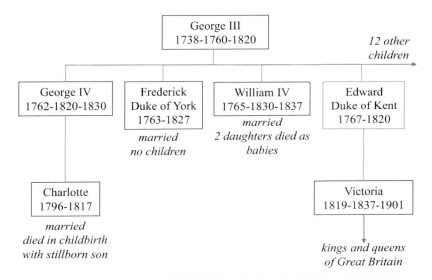

Chart shows the monarchs of Great Britain from George III to Queen Victoria.
George III was succeeded in 1820 by his eldest son as George IV.
George IV was succeeded in 1830 by his second brother as William IV. George IV's only child, Princess Charlotte, and his first brother, Frederick Duke of York, had both died before him.
William IV had ten illegitimate children with the actress Mrs Jordan, but no surviving children from his marriage. He was succeeded in 1837 by his niece Victoria, the only child of his next brother Edward Duke of Kent who had died when she was a baby.

3. FROM RICHARD OF CORNWALL TO THE BLACK PRINCE
THE ROYAL EARLS AND DUKES OF CORNWALL

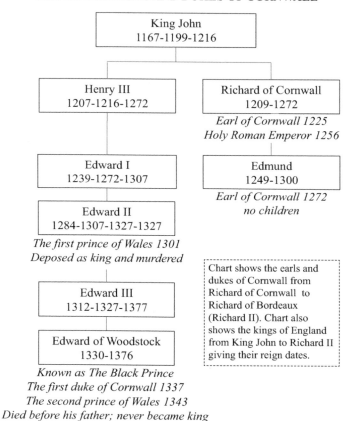

King John
1167-1199-1216

Henry III
1207-1216-1272

Richard of Cornwall
1209-1272

Earl of Cornwall 1225
Holy Roman Emperor 1256

Edward I
1239-1272-1307

Edmund
1249-1300

Earl of Cornwall 1272
no children

Edward II
1284-1307-1327-1327

The first prince of Wales 1301
Deposed as king and murdered

Chart shows the earls and
dukes of Cornwall from
Richard of Cornwall to
Richard of Bordeaux
(Richard II). Chart also
shows the kings of England
from King John to Richard II
giving their reign dates.

Edward III
1312-1327-1377

Edward of Woodstock
1330-1376

Known as The Black Prince
The first duke of Cornwall 1337
The second prince of Wales 1343
Died before his father; never became king

Richard of Bordeaux later Richard II
1367-1377-1399-1400

Duke of Cornwall by special creation 1376-1377
Deposed as king and starved himself to death

4. THE TWENTY-FOUR ROYAL DUKES OF CORNWALL

This chart lists the dukes of Cornwall and their duchesses from the time the duchy was created in 1337 up to the present day with a brief pen picture of each duke. It also lists the periods when there was no duke in existence and the duchy was held by the crown. It is difficult to be precise about the number of dukes who have held the title. A duke of Cornwall is born not created and in theory a baby born who lives only briefly still holds the title. This list shows twenty-four dukes including two sons of Henry VIII and one of Charles I who died as tiny babies. The list shows that only ten princesses have held the title duchess of Cornwall. Many of the dukes of Cornwall died unmarried or were married only after they came to the throne and no longer held the title.

1.   Edward of Woodstock (1330-1376), later known as The Black Prince
Duke of Cornwall 1337-1376

Son of King Edward III.
The first duke when the duchy was created in 1337 and the fourth longest serving (thirty-nine years)
Victor of Crecy and Poitiers he was the model of English chivalry
Married, as her third husband, **Joan of Kent (the first duchess of Cornwall)**
Held his court at Restormel Castle in 1354 and 1362/3
Died before his father and never became king

2.   Richard of Bordeaux (1367-1400), later King Richard II
Duke of Cornwall 1376-1377

Son of the Black Prince he did not inherit his father's military talents
The only duke of Cornwall to hold the title by special creation following his father's death as the grandson and heir (rather than the son) of Edward III
Married twice after becoming king in 1377 but had no children
Deposed by Henry IV in 1399 and starved himself to death in confinement

1377-1399: twenty-two-year vacancy – the duchy reverted to the crown

3. Henry of Monmouth (1387-1422), later King Henry V
Duke of Cornwall 1399-1413

Son of Henry IV (the first king from the house of Lancaster)
Became duke of Cornwall after his father usurped the throne from Richard II
Warrior king and victor of Agincourt
Married after becoming king in 1413 on the death of his father

1413-1421: eight-year vacancy – the duchy reverted to the crown

4. Henry of the house of Lancaster (1421-1471) later Henry VI
Duke of Cornwall 1421-1422
Son of Henry V he was the first duke to be born as duke of Cornwall
Succeeded his father as king at a few months old
Was also the (disputed) heir to the throne of France and inherited mental illness from his grandfather King Charles VI of France
The Wars of the Roses (the house of Lancaster against the house of York) began during his reign
Deposed twice for the Yorkist King Edward IV and murdered in confinement

1422-1453: thirty-one-year vacancy – the duchy reverted to the crown

5. Edward of Westminster (1453-1471)
Duke of Cornwall 1453-1471
Son of Henry VI he was duke of Cornwall from birth, but his title was disputed by the house of York
*Married **Anne Neville (second duchess of Cornwall)** the daughter of Earl Warwick the Kingmaker; her second husband was King Richard III*
Never became king; killed aged seventeen at the Battle of Tewkesbury during the Wars of the Roses; two weeks later his father was murdered

6. Edward of the Sanctuary (1470-1483?), briefly King Edward V
Duke of Cornwall 1471-1483
Son of Edward IV he became duke of Cornwall when his father regained the throne at the Battle of Tewkesbury in 1471
Succeeded his father as king in 1483 but was deposed two months later by his uncle Richard III
With his younger brother Richard was imprisoned in the Tower of London and murdered soon after; they are history's famous Princes in the Tower

7. Edward of Middleham (1473-1484)
Duke of Cornwall 1483-1484
Only child of Richard III and Anne Neville he became duke of Cornwall after his father usurped the throne in 1483
Died at ten years old

1484-1486: two-year vacancy – the duchy reverted to the crown

8. Arthur Tudor (1486-1502)
Duke of Cornwall 1486-1502
Son of Henry VII (the first Tudor king who defeated Richard III at the Battle of
Bosworth Field in 1485 to end the Wars of the Roses)
Was duke of Cornwall from his birth
The pretender Perkin Warbeck launched a claim to the throne during his tenancy
*Married **Catherine of Aragon (the third duchess of Cornwall)** whose second*
husband was his younger brother Henry VIII
Died aged fifteen and never became king

9. Henry Tudor (1491-1547) later King Henry VIII
Duke of Cornwall 1502-1509
Younger son of Henry VII, he succeeded his elder brother Arthur as duke
This raised questions about whether the title could pass to the eldest surviving
(rather than eldest born) son of the sovereign
Married Catherine of Aragon as her second husband after his accession as king

1509-1511: two-year vacancy – the duchy reverted to the crown

10. Henry infant son of Henry VIII (born and died 1511)
Duke of Cornwall briefly 1511
The son of Henry VIII and Catherine of Aragon died at eight weeks old

1511-1514: three-year vacancy – the duchy reverted to the crown

11. Henry second infant son of Henry VIII (born and died 1514)
Duke of Cornwall briefly 1514
The son of Henry VIII and Catherine of Aragon died on the same day he was born
His existence is mentioned in some but not all sources

1514-1537: twenty-three-year vacancy – the duchy reverted to the crown

12. Edward Tudor (1537-1553) later King Edward VI
Duke of Cornwall 1537-1547
The son of Henry VIII and Jane Seymour he was born as duke of Cornwall
Succeeded his father as king but died unmarried aged fifteen

1547-1603: forty-seven-year vacancy – the duchy reverted to the crown

13. Henry Frederick Stuart (1594-1612)
Duke of Cornwall 1603-1612

The son of James I (the first of the Stuart line of sovereigns)
Became duke of Cornwall when his father succeeded Queen Elizabeth I
Showed great promise but died unmarried at eighteen and never became king

14. Charles Stuart (1600-1649) later King Charles I
Duke of Cornwall 1612-1625

The younger son of James I became duke on the death of his elder brother
Visited Cornwall after he became king on campaign during the English Civil War (1642-1651)
An unsuccessful king he was executed by parliament in 1649

1625-1629: four-year vacancy – the duchy reverted to the crown

15. Charles infant son of Charles I (born and died 1629)
Duke of Cornwall briefly 1629

The eldest son of Charles I died on the same day he was born.

1629-1630: one-year vacancy – the duchy reverted to the crown

16. Charles Stuart (1630-1685) later Charles II
Duke of Cornwall 1630-1649

The son of Charles I he was duke of Cornwall from birth until his father's execution in 1649
Spent time in Cornwall while duke during the English Civil War and escaped to France from Falmouth in 1646
Restored to the throne in 1660 after the Civil War

1649-1660: the interregnum period with no monarchy

1660-1688: twenty-eight-year vacancy – the duchy reverted to the crown

17. James Francis Edward Stuart (1688-1766) later known as the Old Pretender
Duke of Cornwall 1688

The son of James II his birth was the catalyst for the Glorious Revolution of 1688 when his father was deposed
Spent his life in exile from where he launched abortive attempts to regain the throne (1715 and 1745)
Founder of the line of Jacobin (or Stuart) claimants to the British throne

1688-1714: twenty-five-year vacancy – the duchy reverted to the crown

18. George Augustus (1683-1760) later King George II
Duke of Cornwall 1714-1727

Son of George I (the first Hanoverian king) and the imprisoned Sophie Dorothee of Celle
Became duke of Cornwall when his father succeeded Queen Anne
Born in Hannover (where his father was duke) and came to England only as an adult
*Married **Caroline of Ansbach (the fourth duchess of Cornwall)***

19. Frederick Lewis (1707-1751)
Duke of Cornwall 1727-1751

The son of George II he was born in Hannover and came to England only as an adult
*Married **Augusta of Saxe-Gotha-Altenburg (the fifth duchess of Cornwall)***
Died before his father and never became king
The father of George III

1751-1762: eleven-year vacancy – the duchy reverted to the crown

20. George (1762-1830) later Prince Regent and then King George IV
Duke of Cornwall 1762-1820

The son of George III he was born duke of Cornwall and became the third longest serving (fifty-seven years)
Talented and charming but profligate and debauched
Continued the Hanoverian tradition of animosity between father and son
*His marriage to **Caroline of Brunswick (the sixth duchess of Cornwall)** quickly became a disaster*

1820-1841: twenty-one-year vacancy – the duchy reverted to the crown

21. Albert Edward (1841-1910) known as Bertie later King Edward VII
Duke of Cornwall 1841-1901

The son of Queen Victoria he was the first monarch of the Saxe-Coburg and Gotha line
Born as duke he became the second longest serving (fifty-nine years)
Only the third duke known to have visited Cornwall when he came as a child on the royal visit in 1846
His father Prince Albert revamped the administration and finances of the duchy during his minority
*Married **Alexandra of Denmark (the seventh duchess)***
Popular with the public but denied any useful role by his mother

22. George (1865-1936) later King George V
Duke of Cornwall 1901-1910
The eldest surviving son of Edward VII became duke when his father succeeded to the throne
Married **Mary of Teck (the eighth duchess of Cornwall)**
Changed the surname of the royal family to 'Windsor' during World War I

23. Edward (1894-1972) later King Edward VIII and the duke of Windsor
Duke of Cornwall 1910-1936
The son of George V became duke on the accession of his father
Glamorous and popular he wanted to do good but suffered from a sense of entitlement and lacked staying power
Succeeded as king in 1936 but abdicated the throne later the same year to marry Wallis Simpson

1936-1952: sixteen-year vacancy – the duchy reverted to the crown

24. Charles (born 1948)
Duke of Cornwall 1952 to date
Became duke on the accession of his mother as Queen Elizabeth II.
The longest serving duke of Cornwall (seventy years and still counting).
Current beneficiary of the enormous revenues and special privileges of the duchy.
Married (1) **Diana Spencer (the ninth duchess of Cornwall)** *and (2)* **Camilla Parker-Bowles (the tenth duchess of Cornwall).**

5. THE EDGCUMBES AT COTEHELE AND MOUNT EDGCUMBE

William Edgcumbe
d 1379/80

Married 1353 Hillaria Cotehele, the heiress of Cotehele

Sir Richard Edgcumbe I
1443 - 1489

Great-grandson of William and Hillaria (two generations omitted)
Knighted at Bosworth Field 1485
Favoured courtier of King Henry VII
Re-built Cotehele

Sir Piers Edgcumbe I
1468 - 1539

Married 1493 Joan Durnford, the heiress of Mount Edgcumbe
Enclosed a deer park at Mount Edgcumbe in 1515

Sir Richard Edgcumbe II
c1497 – 1562

Built Mount Edgcumbe House that then became the main family residence

Colonel Sir Piers Edgcumbe III
c1610 - 1666

Great-grandson of Sir Richard Edgcumbe II (two generations omitted)
Moved to Cotehele during the English Civil War and made changes to the internal lay-out

Lord Richard Edgcumbe I
1680 – 1758

Grandson of Colonel Sir Piers Edgcumbe III (one generation omitted)
Promoted to baron in the peerage 1742
Close associate of Prime Minister Horace Walpole
Patron of Sir Joshua Reynolds
Remodelled Mount Edgcumbe House and gardens

Lord Richard Edgcumbe II
1716 – 1761

Black sheep of the family
Died unmarried and was succeeded by his brother

Lord George Mount Edgcumbe 1721 – 1795	*Created first viscount 1781; first earl Mount Edgcumbe 1789* *Hosted George III and Queen Charlotte at Mount Edgcumbe in 1781 and 1789*
Lord Ernest Augustus Mount Edgcumbe 1797 – 1861	*The third earl* *Grandson of Lord George Mount Edgcumbe (one generation omitted)* *Queen Victoria's host at Mount Edgcumbe during the royal visit to Cornwall in 1846*
Lord William Henry Mount Edgcumbe 1832 – 1917	*The fourth earl* *Senior courtier to Queen Victoria and to King Edward VII (Bertie)* *The last earl to be succeeded by his son*
Lord Piers Alexander Mount Edgcumbe 1865 – 1944	*The fifth and last earl of the senior line* *Succeeded by a second cousin*
Lord Kenelm Mount Edgcumbe 1873 – 1965	*The sixth earl* *Transferred Cotehele to the National Trust in 1947* *Re-built Mount Edgcumbe after it was destroyed in World War II* *Succeeded by a cousin*
Lord Edward Piers Mount Edgcumbe 1903 - 1982	*The seventh earl and first of the New Zealand earls* *Sold Mount Edgcumbe to Cornwall County Council and Plymouth City Council in 1971*
Lord Robert Mount Edgcumbe 1939 – 2021	*The eighth earl and second New Zealand earl* *The last earl to live in Mount Edgcumbe House*

Source: *Cotehele: A Souvenir Guide*. National Trust, 2013, inside front cover.

6. THE MOUNT EDGCUMBE SUCCESSION

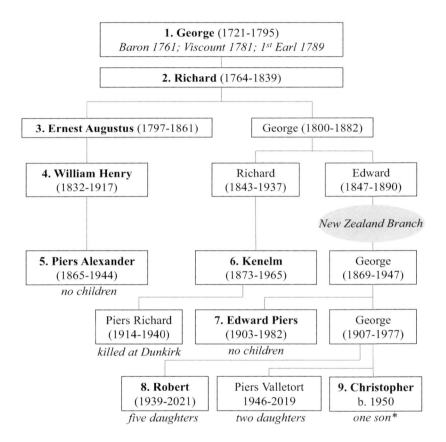

1. George (1721-1795)
Baron 1761; Viscount 1781; 1ˢᵗ Earl 1789

2. Richard (1764-1839)

3. Ernest Augustus (1797-1861)

George (1800-1882)

4. William Henry (1832-1917)

Richard (1843-1937)

Edward (1847-1890)

New Zealand Branch

5. Piers Alexander (1865-1944)
no children

6. Kenelm (1873-1965)

George (1869-1947)

Piers Richard (1914-1940)
killed at Dunkirk

7. Edward Piers (1903-1982)
no children

George (1907-1977)

8. Robert (1939-2021)
five daughters

Piers Valletort 1946-2019
two daughters

9. Christopher b. 1950
one son*

Chart shows the earls of Mount Edgcumbe since the earldom was created in 1789. The nine earls are shown in bold text. Chart shows how the senior line died out with the 5ᵗʰ earl in 1944 and later earls descended from a younger brother of the 3ʳᵈ earl. The 7ᵗʰ earl was the first from the New Zealand branch. Information on the 9ᵗʰ earl and his heir* Douglas George Valletort born in 1985 from www.thepeerage.com . Not all family members are shown.

7. THE ST AUBYNS AT ST MICHAEL'S MOUNT

Colonel John St Aubyn
1610 -1684

Purchased St Michael's Mount in 1659
Allegedly swept off the causeway and died

Sir John St Aubyn I
1645 – 1699

The first baronet 1671

Sir John St Aubyn II
1669 – 1714

Second baronet

Sir John St Aubyn III
1700 – 1744

Third baronet

Sir John St Aubyn IV
1726 – 1772

Fourth baronet
Created the Blue Drawing Rooms

Sir John St Aubyn V
1758 – 1839

Fifth baronet
Had fifteen illegitimate children but no
legitimate heir, so the baronetcy ended
Married his long-standing partner Juliana
Vinicombe in 1822

James St Aubyn
1783 – 1862

Eldest illegitimate son of the fifth baronet
Succeeded by his brother

Sir Edward St Aubyn
1799 – 1872

Created baronet in 1866

Lord John St Levan I
1829 – 1908

Created baron in 1887
Built the east wing; re-built the village;
laid a stone causeway

Lord John St Levan II
1857 – 1940

Second baron

Lord Francis St Levan
1895 – 1978

Third Baron
Donated St Michael's Mount to the
National Trust in 1954

Lord John St Levan III
1919 – 2013

Fourth baron

Lord James St Levan
b 1950

Fifth baron
The current incumbent

Source: *A Personal Tour of St Michael's Mount.* James and Mary St Aubyn, 2010, 40.

8. THE KILLIGREWS OF ARWENACK FALMOUTH

John Killigrew I
died 1567

The first governor of Pendennis Castle
Rebuilt Arwenack House

Sir John Killigrew II
died 1584

Second governor of Pendennis Castle
With his father imprisoned for piracy during the reign of the Catholic Queen Mary 1
Knighted by the Protestant Queen Elizabeth I (Mary's sister) in 1574

Sir John Killigrew III
1554 – 1605

Third governor of Pendennis Castle until sacked in 1598
Suspected of taking a bribe to hand over Pendennis to the Spanish
Mired in debt and died in prison

Sir John Killigrew IV
1583-1633

With his brother founded the town of Falmouth on a site next to Arwenack
Divorced in an acrimonious divorce battle
No children

Sir Peter Killigrew
1593-1667

Younger brother of John Killigrew IV
Royalist (supporter of the king) in the Civil War
Obtained a royal charter for Falmouth in 1661 after the restoration

Sir Peter Killigrew II
1634-1705

The last of the male line: his son George having predeceased him

Martin Lister Killigrew
1666-1745

The husband of Anne Killigrew, daughter of Sir Peter Killigrew II
Added Killigrew to his surname in a failed attempt to perpetuate the family line
No children
Erected a granite obelisk at Arwenack in 1737 in honour of his wife's family

Sources: Crispin Gill, *The Great Cornish families: A History of the People and their Houses*. Paul Pattison, *Pendennis Castle and St Mawes Castle*. *Killigrew Obelisk at Arwenack House*. Wikipedia, *Arwenack*. www.falmouth.co.uk.

9. THE TREFFRYS OF PLACE HOUSE FOWEY

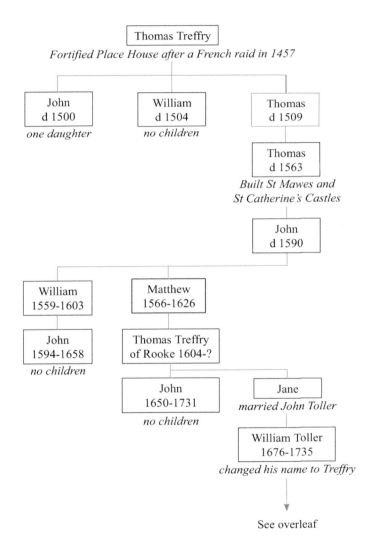

Thomas Treffry
Fortified Place House after a French raid in 1457

John
d 1500
one daughter

William
d 1504
no children

Thomas
d 1509

Thomas
d 1563
*Built St Mawes and
St Catherine's Castles*

John
d 1590

William
1559-1603

Matthew
1566-1626

John
1594-1658
no children

Thomas Treffry
of Rooke 1604-?

John
1650-1731
no children

Jane
married John Toller

William Toller
1676-1735
changed his name to Treffry

See overleaf

153

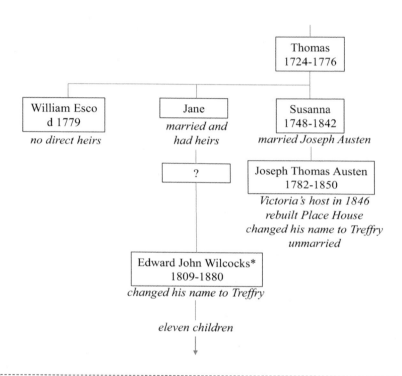

Chart shows extracts from the family tree of the Treffrys of Place House, Fowey from the 16th to the 19th centuries based on the sources indicated. It shows how Place three times descended through the female line. (*Edward John Wilcocks was the heir of Joseph Thomas (Austen) Treffry.)

Sources: Crispin Gill, *The Great Cornish Families: A History of the People and Their Houses.* A L Rowse, *The Little Land of Cornwall.*

NOTES

Chapter 1. Introduction
1. *The Illustrated London News*, September 12, 1846.
2. RA VIC/MAIN/QVJ (W) 5 September 1846 (Princess Beatrice's copies). Retrieved 17 March 2022.
3. RA VIC/MAIN/QVJ (W) 22 August 1846 (Princess Beatrice's copies). Retrieved 17 March 2022.
4. RA VIC/MAIN/QVJ (W) 21 August 1846 (Princess Beatrice's copies). Retrieved 17 March 2022.
5. RA VIC/MAIN/QVJ (W) 9 September 1846 (Princess Beatrice's copies). Retrieved 17 March 2022.
6. Roger Fulford (edited), *Dearest Child, Private Correspondence of Queen Victoria and the Princess Royal, 1858-1861*. London: Evans Brothers, 1964, 78. Letter from Queen Victoria to the newly married Vicky, 24 March 1858.
7. See Susan Symons, *Schloss in Thuringia: The Fascinating Royal History of German Castles*. St Just-in-Roseland: Roseland Books, 2021, 72-74.
8. Richard Linzey, *The Castles of Pendennis and St Mawes*. London: English Heritage, 1999, 24.
9. The coins are bezants (Byzantine gold coins) and thought to be a reference to Richard Earl of Cornwall who went on crusade in 1240.

Chapter 2. The royal yacht Victoria and Albert
1. D Phillips-Birt, *Sovereigns of the Seas: Royal Steam Yachts*. Country Life: May 26, 1977, 1460.
2. Linda Batchelor, *Queen Victoria visits Falmouth*. The Bartlett Maritime Research Centre, National Maritime Museum, Falmouth: 2021.
3. RA VIC/MAIN/QVJ(W) Tuesday 8 August 1843 (Princess Beatrice's copies) retrieved 9 September 2021.
4. RA VIC/MAIN/QVJ (W) 28 August 1843 (Princess Beatrice's copies) and RA VIC/MAIN/QVJ (W) 1 September 1843 (Princess Beatrice's copies). Retrieved 17 March 2022.
5. Kate Hubbard, *Serving Victoria: Life in the Royal Household*. London: Chatto and Windus, 2012, 88.
6. Philip Whitwell Wilson (edited), *The Greville Diary: Including Pages Hitherto Withheld from Publication*. New York: Doubleday Page, 1927, 245-246.
7. Anonymous, *A Diary of Royal Movements and of Personal Events and Incidents in the Life and Reign of Her Most Gracious Majesty Queen Victoria: Compiled from Official Documents and Public Records, Volume the First*. London: Elliot Stock, 1883. Reprinted by Franklin Classics, 234.

8. Anonymous, *A Diary of Royal Movements*, 237. Batchelor, *Queen Victoria visits Falmouth*.

9. Victoire of Saxe-Coburg and Gotha (1822-1857), married to Louis, duke of Nemours (1814-1896), was the daughter of a younger brother of Victoria's mother and Albert's father.

10. K. D. Reynolds, *Fitzclarence, Lord Adolphus (1802-1856)*. Oxford Dictionary of National Biography: published online 23 September 2004.

11. RA VIC/MAIN/QVJ (W) 23 January 1838 (Lord Esher's typescript). Retrieved 18 March 2022.

12. RA VIC/MAIN/QVJ (W) 30 August 1843 (Princess Beatrice's copies). Retrieved 17 March 2022.

13. RA VIC/MAIN/QVJ (W) 4 September 1843 (Princess Beatrice's copies). Retrieved 18 March 2022.

14. RA VIC/MAIN/QVJ (W) 22 August 1846 (Princess Beatrice's copies). Retrieved 17 March 2022.

Chapter 3. The royal visit day by day

1. The names Victoria mentions in her journal include Lady Frances Jocelyn, Miss Napier and Miss Lucy Kerr (lady in waiting and maids of honour); Lord Spencer, Lord Alfred Paget and Colonel Grey (gentleman in waiting and equerries); Mademoiselle Charrier and Fraulein Grüner (governesses); George Anson (Albert's private secretary); Sir James Clark (the royal doctor); Lord Palmerston (foreign secretary); Lord Adolphus Fitzclarence (captain of the royal yacht *Victoria and Albert*); and Captain Crispin (presumably in command of another ship in the royal flotilla).

2. Roger Fulford, *The Prince Consort*. London: Macmillan, 1966, 51.

3. Royal Collection Trust, RCIN 450803.

4. RA VIC/MAIN/QVJ (W) 21 August 1846 (Princess Beatrice's copies). Retrieved 17 March 2022.

5. Royal Collection Trust, RCIN 920177.

6. *Cothele on the Banks of the Tamar, the Ancient Seat of The R[t] Hon[ble] The Earl of Mount Edgcumbe* by Nicholas Condy with a descriptive account written expressly for the work by the Rev[d] F. V. J. Arundell.

7. See Cynthia Gaskell Brown, *Images of Mount Edgcumbe Cornwall*. Plymouth: Western Morning News, 2000, 22-33.

8. RA VIC/MAIN/QVJ (W) 22 August 1846 (Princess Beatrice's copies). Retrieved 17 March 2022.

9. RA VIC/MAIN/QVJ (W) 24 August 1846 (Princess Beatrice's copies). Retrieved 19 March 2022.

10. RA VIC/MAIN/QVJ (W) 29 August 1846 (Princess Beatrice's copies). Retrieved 19 March 2022.

11. A M. Broadley, *The Boyhood of a Great King 1841-1858: An Account of the Early Years of the Life of His Majesty Edward VII*. London: Harper and Brothers, 1906, 189. Bertie wore his sailor suit for the first time at Osborne for his father's birthday on 26 August 1846.

12. Royal Collection Trust, RCIN 980054.

13. RA VIC/MAIN/QVJ (W) 6 September 1846 (Princess Beatrice's copies). Retrieved 19 March 2022.

14. John St Aubyn, *St Michael's Mount: Illustrated History and Guide*. John St Aubyn, 1978. From the section headed 'Place of Pilgrimage'. This guidebook has no page numbers.

15. James St Aubyn, *A Personal Tour of St Michael's Mount*. James and Mary St Aubyn, 2010, 24.

16. *The Illustrated London News*, September 12, 1846.

17. Linda Batchelor, *Queen Victoria visits Falmouth*. The Bartlett Maritime Research Centre, National Maritime Museum, Falmouth: 2021.

18. Wikipedia King Harry Ferry references a poll by *The Independent* newspaper of the world's top ten scenic ferry trips.

19. RA VIC/MAIN/QVJ (W) 7 September 1846 (Princess Beatrice's copies). Retrieved 19 March 2022.

20. Batchelor, *Queen Victoria visits Falmouth*.

21. Ibid, quoting Charles Fox, *Glendurgan: A Personal Memoir of a Garden in Cornwall*. Penzance: Alison Hodge, 2004.

22. RA VIC/MAIN/QVJ (W) 8 September 1846 (Princess Beatrice's copies). Retrieved 19 March 2022.

23. *The Illustrated London News*, September 19,1846.

24. Tony Brooks, *A History of Iron Mining in Cornwall*. St Austell: Cornish Hillside Publications, 2011, 33.

25. *The Illustrated London News*, September 19,1846.

26. Crispin Gill, *The Great Cornish Families: A History of the People and their Houses*. Wellington: Halsgrove, 2011, 85.

27. *The Illustrated London News*, September 19,1846.

Chapter 4. Cotehele and Mount Edgcumbe

1. RA VIC/MAIN/QVJ (W) 21 August 1846 (Princess Beatrice's copies). Retrieved 17 March 2022.

2. Richard Carew, *The Survey of Cornwall: Written by Richard Carew of Antonie, Esquire*. First published 1602/1603. Reprinted 2004 by Tamar Books, Launceston, Cornwall, 134.

3. Frank Ernest Halliday, *A History of Cornwall*. Looe: House of Stratus, 2009, 181.

4. Crispin Gill. *The Great Cornish families: A History of the People and their Houses*. Wellington: Halsgrove, 2011, 26.

5. Lady Margaret Denny (her married name) 1560-1648 was the daughter of Sir Piers Edgcumbe II (1535-1607), the grandson of the first Sir Piers.

6. *Cothele on the Banks of the Tamar, the Ancient Seat of the Rt. Hon'ble The Earl of Mount Edgcumbe*. By Nicholas Condy with a descriptive account written expressly for the work by the Rev'd F.V.J. Arundell.

7. The booklets were removed, hopefully temporarily, during the covid 19 pandemic.

8. Extract from Queen Charlotte's journal entry for her visit. Quoted in Rachael Hunt, *Cotehele: A Souvenir Guide*. National Trust, 2013, 22.

9. Visitor information at Cotehele.

10. Gill, *The Great Cornish families*, 28.

11. Cynthia Gaskell Brown, *Mount Edgcumbe House and Country Park*. Torpoint Cornwall: Mount Edgcumbe House and Country Park, 1998, 18.

12. *History and Guide to Mount Edgcumbe House and Country Park*. Cornwall County Council and Plymouth City Council: [1970s?], 9.

13. Gaskell Brown, *Mount Edgcumbe House and Country Park*, 19.

14. Bill Scolding, *Five Walks Around Mount Edgcumbe and the Rame Peninsula*. Cornwall County Council 2007, 8.

15. RA VIC/MAIN/QVJ (W) 31 August 1843 (Princess Beatrice's copies). Retrieved 17 March 2022.

16. RA VIC/MAIN/QVJ(W) Thursday 29 April 1858 (Princess Beatrice's copies) retrieved 17 September 2021.

17. Giles St Aubyn, *Edward VII: Prince and King*. London: William Collins Sons & Co Ltd 1979, 39-41.

18. Visitor information at Cotehele.

19. Ibid.

20. Hunt, *Cotehele*, 8.

21. Ibid, 32. The words are those of Earl Kenelm's daughter Hilaria.

22. The mechanics were that the owner donated the property to the National Trust and the National Land Fund reimbursed the Inland Revenue for the inheritance tax foregone.

23. Guided tour at Mount Edgcumbe House.

24. www.thepeerage.com

25. Guided tour at Mount Edgcumbe House.

Chapter 5. St Michael's Mount and Kynance Cove

1. www.stmichaelsmount.co.uk
2. Cecil Woodham-Smith, *Queen Victoria Her Life and Times: Volume I, 1819 – 1861*. London: Hamish Hamilton, 1972, 210. Letter from Prince Albert to Prince Wilhelm von Löwenstein, May 1840.
3. John St Aubyn, *St Michael's Mount: Illustrated History and Guide*. John St Aubyn: 1978, section headed 'Perkin Warbeck's Rebellion 1497 – Leaves Wife at Mount' (this book has no page numbers).
4. Alison Weir, *Richard III and The Princes in The Tower*. London: Vintage Books, 2014, 239-242. Ms Weir discusses the various possibilities raised by historians but concludes that the pretender probably was, as he confessed, Perkin Warbeck.
5. St Aubyn, *St Michael's Mount*, section headed 'Perkin Warbeck's Rebellion 1497'.
6. Ibid, 'section headed 'The Mount as a Private House'.
7. Wikipedia: *Chevy Chase*.
8. RA VIC/MAIN/QVJ (W) 6 September 1846 (Princess Beatrice's copies). Retrieved 19 March 2022.
9. James St Aubyn, *A Personal Tour of St Michael's Mount*. James and Mary St Aubyn, 2010, 27. Also, information available for visitors on St Michael's Mount.
10. St Aubyn, *St Michael's Mount*, section headed 'Victorian and Modern'.
11. St Aubyn, *A Personal Tour of St Michael's Mount*, 9.
12. Ibid.
13. St Aubyn, *St Michael's Mount*, section headed 'Victorian and Modern'.
14. Giles St Aubyn, *Queen Victoria: A Portrait* and *Edward VII: Prince and King*.
15. St Aubyn, *A Personal Tour of St Michael's Mount*, 7.
16. www.officialdata.org ONS CPI inflation calculator; £100k in 1873 is equivalent to £11,419k in 2021.
17. www.nationaltrust.org.uk/kynance-cove
18. RA VIC/MAIN/QVJ (W) 6 September 1846 (Princess Beatrice's copies). Retrieved 19 March 2022.
19. Michael Sagar-Fenton with Stuart B. Smith, *Serpentine*. Truro: Truran, 2005, 18.
20. Ibid, 19.
21. Ibid 37, 39.
22. Wikipedia. *St Grada and Holy Cross Church, Grade*. Source: 'Reopening of the Parish Church of Grade', Royal Cornwall Gazette, 3 July 1863.

Chapter 6. Pendennis Castle Falmouth and St Mawes Castle

1. *The Illustrated London News*, September 12, 1846.

2. *The Life and Times of Queen Victoria*. London: Cassell and Company, 1901, Volume I, 266.

3. Philip Whitwell Wilson (edited), *The Greville Diary: Including Pages Hitherto Withheld from Publication*. New York: Doubleday Page & Company, 1927, 455. Greville had been talking to Lady Sarah Lyttelton who was appointed superintendent in charge of the royal nursery in 1842.

4. Hibbert, *Queen Victoria in Her Letters and Journals*, 93. Letter from Queen Victoria to King Leopold of Belgium 29 November 1841. 'You will understand how fervent my prayers ... to see him resemble his angelic dearest Father in every, every respect, both in body and mind.'

5. Woodham-Smith, *Queen Victoria Her Life and Times*, 267 and 458, quoting a memorandum by Baron Stockmar of 28 July 1846. Stockmar's guiding role as mentor to the royal family began when he was appointed private secretary to Prince Leopold of Saxe-Coburg and Gotha (the uncle of both Victoria and Albert). Stockmar was with Prince Leopold when his first wife, Princess Charlotte of Wales, tragically died in childbirth in 1817 and Stockmar advised Leopold on the offer of the Belgian crown in 1831 (he accepted). In the tense months before Victoria succeeded to the British throne in June 1837 uncle Leopold sent Stockmar to advise his niece. Stockmar returned to England with Albert on his marriage and continued to advise the royal couple.

6. Wilson (edited), *The Greville Diary*, 455. Charles Greville was clerk to the privy council during the reigns of George IV, William IV, and Queen Victoria.

7. Elizabeth Longford, *Queen Victoria*. London: The Folio Society, 2007, 202.

8. Called *the Truce of Nice* this ended the Italian War of 1536-1538 between Francis I and Charles V over control of territory in northern Italy.

9. Paul Pattison, *Pendennis Castle and St Mawes Castle*. London: English Heritage, 2009, 26.

10. RA VIC/MAIN/QVJ (W) 5 September 1846 (Princess Beatrice's copies). Retrieved 17 March 2022.

11. Richard Carew, *The Survey of Cornwall: Written by Richard Carew of Antonie, Esquire*. First published 1602/1603. Reprinted 2004 by Tamar Books, Launceston, Cornwall, 180.

12. Richard Linzey, *The Castles of Pendennis and St Mawes*. London: English Heritage, 1999, 26.

13. Crispin Gill, *The Great Cornish families: A History of the People and their Houses*. Wellington: Halsgrove, 2011, 55.

14. Ibid, 53.
15. Modern plaque on the obelisk outside Arwenack erected by Martin Lister Killigrew in 1737.
16. Carew, *The Survey of Cornwall*, 180.
17. Helen McCabe, *Houses and Gardens of Cornwall: A Personal Choice*. Padstow: Tabb House, 1988, 102.
18. www.falmouth.co.uk
19. Gill, *The Great Cornish families*, 56.
20. Ruth Norrington, *My Dearest Minette: Letters Between Charles II and his Sister the Duchesse d'Orléans*. London: Peter Owen, 1996, 12.
21. Letter from Queen Henrietta Maria to King Charles I, Exeter 28 June 1644. Quoted in Norrington, *My Dearest Minette*, 14.
22. Queen Henrietta Maria's escape from Pendennis is excitingly described in Linda Batchelor, *Royal Escape from Falmouth*. The Bartlett Maritime Research Centre, National Maritime Museum, Falmouth: 2021.
23. Norrington, *My Dearest Minette*, 19.
24. Batchelor, *Royal Escape from Falmouth*.
25. Antonia Fraser, *King Charles II*. London: Weidenfeld and Nicholson, 1979, 41.
26. Frank Ernest Halliday, *A History of Cornwall*. Looe: House of Stratus, 2009, 258.
27. Ibid, 259.
28. Pattison, *Pendennis Castle and St Mawes Castle*, 40.

Chapter 7. Restormel Castle and Place House Fowey

1. duchyofcornwall.org/history-of-the-duchy
2. Frank Ernest Halliday, *A History of Cornwall*. Looe: House of Stratus, 2009, 156.
3. Nicholas A D Molyneux, *Restormel Castle Cornwall*. English Heritage, 14.
4. E Nesbit and Doris Ashley, *Children's Stories from English History*. Published 1914.
5. The fourteenth century chronicler Jean Froissart quoted in Penny Lawne, *Joan of Kent: The First Princess of Wales*. Stroud: Amberly Publishing, 2016, 6.
6. Michael Jones, *The Black Prince*. London: Head of Zeus, 2017, 132.
7. Halliday, *A History of Cornwall*, 129.
8. Molyneux, *Restormel Castle Cornwall*, 20. The last date they are known to have been at Restormel is 10 April and they sailed from Plymouth in June.
9. Richard Barber, *Edward [Edward of Woodstock; known as the Black Prince], prince of Wales and Aquitaine*. Oxford Dictionary of National Biography published online 23 September 2004.

10. Tony Brooks, *A History of Iron Mining in Cornwall*. St Austell: Cornish Hillside Publications, 2011, 21.

11. RA VIC/MAIN/QVJ (W) 8 September 1846 (Princess Beatrice's copies). Retrieved 19 March 2022.

12. Brooks, *A History of Iron Mining in Cornwall*, 34. Published in the Royal Cornwall Gazette 22 August 1851. Victoria's journal entry for that day states that she and Albert walked the half mile from Restormel Castle to the mine as does the report in *The Illustrated London News* on 19 September 1846. The mine captain's description of the visit says the queen and prince arrived at the mine in a 'chay' or light carriage. His account did not appear in the newspaper until five years later (22 August 1851) so perhaps is less reliable.

13. Ibid, 33. Published in the Royal Cornwall Gazette 25 September 1846.

14. *The Life and Times of Queen Victoria*. London: Cassell and Company, 1901, Volume I, 265.

15. Brooks, *A History of Iron Mining in Cornwall*, 34 quoting the mine captain's account published on 22 August 1851.

16. Ibid, 35.

17. Crispin Gill, *The Great Cornish Families: A History of the People and their Houses*. Wellington: Halsgrove, 2011, 82.

18. Ibid.

19. Richard Carew, *The Survey of Cornwall: Written by Richard Carew of Antonie, Esquire*. First published 1602/1603. Reprinted 2004 by Tamar Books, Launceston, Cornwall, 160.

20. Ibid, 158. I have paraphrased Carew's words. He wrote that it was 'a walk which, if I could as plainly show you as myself have oftentimes delightfully seen it, you might and would avow the same to be a place of diversified pleasings.'.

21. Gill, *The Great Cornish Families*, 58.

22. A. L. Rowse, *The Little Land of Cornwall*. Gloucester: Alan Sutton, 1986, 129.

23. Gill, *The Great Cornish Families*, 85.

24. Country Life October 15 1998, *Place Fowey, Cornwall* by Jeremy Musson, 67.

25. www.officialdata.org ONS CPI inflation calculator; £120k in 1846 is equivalent to £14,906k in 2022.

26. RA VIC/MAIN/QVJ (W) 8 September 1846 (Princess Beatrice's copies). Retrieved 19 March 2022.

27. Country Life, *Place Fowey, Cornwall*, 67.

28. *The Illustrated London News*, 19 September 1846.

29. Country Life, *Place Fowey, Cornwall*, 67.

Chapter 8. Return to Osborne House
1. RA VIC/MAIN/QVJ (W) 9 September 1846 (Princess Beatrice's copies). Retrieved 17 March 2022.
2. Roger Fulford, *The Prince Consort*. London: Macmillan 1949, 80.
3. Cecil Woodham-Smith, *Queen Victoria Her Life and Times: Volume I, 1819 – 1861*. London: Hamish Hamilton, 1972, 276. My translation.
4. John Matson, *Dear Osborne: Queen Victoria's Family Life on the Isle of Wight*. London: Hamish Hamilton, 1978, 34 and 159 note 14.
5. Arthur Benson and Viscount Esher (edited), *The Letters of Queen Victoria: 1837-1861*. London: John Murray, 1908, volume II, 41. Letter from Queen Victoria to her uncle King Leopold of the Belgians, Windsor Castle, 25 March 1845.
6. Hermione Hobhouse, *Prince Albert: His Life and Work*. London: Hamish Hamilton, 1983, 117.
7. RA VIC/MAIN/QVJ (W) 14 September 1846 (Princess Beatrice's copies). Retrieved 24 March 2022.
8. Roger Fulford (edited), *Dearest Mama, Private Correspondence of Queen Victoria and the Crown Princess of Prussia 1861-1864*. London: Evans Brothers Ltd, 85. Letter from Queen Victoria to her eldest daughter Vicky written at Osborne 2 July 1862.
9. Matson, *Dear Osborne*, 36 and 159 note 18. Quoting the maid of honour Eleanor Stanley on 27 July 1848.
10. Michael Turner, *Osborne*. London: English Heritage, 2007, 3.
11. Ibid, 35.
12. Ibid, 30.
13. Hobhouse, *Prince Albert*, 130.
14. Matson, *Dear Osborne*, 50.
15. Turner, *Osborne*, 33.
16. Ibid, 20.
17. Roger Fulford (edited), *Dearest Child, Private Correspondence of Queen Victoria and the Princess Royal, 1858-1861*. London: Evans Brothers, 1964, 122. Letter from Queen Victoria to her eldest daughter Vicky written at Osborne 20 July 1858.

Chapter 9. The duchy of Cornwall and its royal dukes
1. Crispin Gill (edited), *The Duchy of Cornwall*. Newton Abbot: David & Charles, 1987, 51.
2. David Burnett, *A Royal Duchy: A Portrait of the Duchy of Cornwall*. Stanbridge Wimborne: The Dovecote Press, 1996, 31-32.
3. Gill (edited), *The Duchy of Cornwall*, 55-56.

4. A. L. Rowse, *The Little Land of Cornwall*. Gloucester: Alan Sutton, 1986, 53.
5. Ibid.
6. duchyofcornwall.org/history-of-the-duchy. This was Thomas Brinton Bishop of Rochester.

BIBLIOGRAPHY

Anonymous. *A Diary of Royal Movements and of Personal Events and Incidents in the Life and Reign of Her Most Gracious Majesty Queen Victoria: Compiled from Official Documents and Public Records, Volume the First.* London: Elliot Stock, 1883. Reprinted by Franklin Classics.

Augusta, Duchess of Saxe-Coburg-Saalfeld. *In Napoleonic Days: Extracts from the Private Diary of Augusta, Duchess of Saxe-Coburg-Saalfeld, Queen Victoria's maternal grandmother, 1806-1821: Selected and Translated by H.R.H. The Princess Beatrice.* London: John Murray, 1941.

Barratt, Rex. *Stately Homes in and Around Truro.* Redruth: Cornish Publications, 1980.

Batchelor Linda. *Queen Victoria visits Falmouth.* The Bartlett Maritime Research Centre, National Maritime Museum, Falmouth: 2021.

Batchelor, Linda. *Royal Escape from Falmouth.* The Bartlett Maritime Research Centre, National Maritime Museum, Falmouth: 2021.

Bates, Robin and Bill Scolding. *Five Walks from the Lizard.* Cornwall County Council, 2001.

Broadley, A M. *The Boyhood of a Great King 1841-1858: An Account of the Early Years of the Life of His Majesty Edward VII.* London: Harper and Brothers, 1906.

Brooks, Tony. *A History of Iron Mining in Cornwall.* St Austell: Cornish Hillside Publications, 2011.

Buckley, J. A. *Medieval Cornish Stannary Charters.* Pool Camborne: Penhellick Publications, 2001.

Burnett, David. *A Royal Duchy: A Portrait of the Duchy of Cornwall.* Stanbridge Wimborne: The Dovecote Press, 1996.

Carew, Richard. *The Survey of Cornwall: Written by Richard Carew of Antonie, Esquire.* First published 1602/1603. Reprinted 2004 by Tamar Books, Launceston, Cornwall.

Duff, David. *Victoria Travels: Journeys of Queen Victoria between 1830 and 1900 with Extracts from her Journal.* London: Frederick Muller, 1970.

Fulford, Roger. *Royal Dukes: Queen Victoria's 'Wicked Uncles'.* London: Pan Books, 1948.

Fulford, Roger (edited). *Dearest Child, Private Correspondence of Queen Victoria and the Princess Royal, 1858-1861.* London: Evans Brothers, 1964.

Gamble, Barry. *Cornwall's Great Houses and Gardens.* Penzance: Alison Hodge Publishers, 2014.

Gaskell Brown, Cynthia. *Mount Edgcumbe House and Country Park.* Torpoint Cornwall: Mount Edgcumbe House and Country Park, 1998.

Gaskell Brown, Cynthia. *Images of Mount Edgcumbe Cornwall*. Plymouth: Western Morning News, 2000.

Gill, Crispin. *The Great Cornish Families: A History of the People and their Houses*. Wellington: Halsgrove, 2011.

Gill, Crispin (edited). *The Duchy of Cornwall*. Newton Abbot: David & Charles, 1987.

Halliday, Frank Ernest. *A History of Cornwall*. Looe: House of Stratus, 2009.

Harvey, John. *The Black Prince and His Age*. Totowa, New Jersey: Rowman and Littlefield, 1976.

Henderson, Charles. *Essays in Cornish History*. Oxford: Oxford University Press, 1935.

Hibbert Christopher. *Queen Victoria in her Letters and Journals: a selection by Christopher Hibbert*. New York: Viking, 1985.

Hobhouse, Hermione. *Prince Albert: His Life and Work*. London: Hamish Hamilton, 1983.

Hubbard, Kate. *Serving Victoria: Life in the Royal Household*. London: Chatto and Windus, 2012.

Hunt, Rachel. *Cotehele: A Souvenir Guide*. National Trust, 2013.

Jones, Michael. *The Black Prince*. London: Head of Zeus, 2017.

Lawne, Penny. *Joan of Kent: The First Princess of Wales*. Stroud: Amberly Publishing, 2016.

Linzey, Richard. *The Castles of Pendennis and St Mawes*. London: English Heritage, 1999.

London, Pete. *Castles of Cornwall and the Scilly Isles*. Redruth: Tor Mark, 2011.

Longford, Elizabeth. *Queen Victoria*. London: The Folio Society, 2007.

Matson, John. *Dear Osborne: Queen Victoria's Family Life on the Isle of Wight*. London: Hamish Hamilton, 1978.

McCabe, Helen. *Houses and Gardens of Cornwall: A Personal Choice*. Padstow: Tabb House, 1988.

Molyneux, Nicholas A D. *Restormel Castle Cornwall*. English Heritage.

Norrington, Ruth. *My Dearest Minette: letters Between Charles II and his Sister the Duchesse d'Orléans*. London: Peter Owen, 1996.

Pasfield Oliver, S. *Pendennis & St Mawes: An Historical Sketch of Two Cornish Castles*. Redruth: Dyllansow Truran Cornish Publications, 1984. Facsimile edition of the original published 1875.

Pattison, Paul. *Pendennis Castle and St Mawes Castle*. London: English Heritage, 2009.

Pennington, Robert R. *A History of the Mining Law of Cornwall and Devon*. Newton Abbot: David & Charles, 1973.

Ridley, Jane. *Bertie: A Life of Edward VII*. London: Chatto and Windus, 2012.

Rowse, A. L. *The Little Land of Cornwall*. Gloucester: Alan Sutton, 1986.

Sagar-Fenton, Michael. *About St Michael's Mount*. Ilkley: Bossiney Books, 1999.

Sagar-Fenton, Michael with Stuart B. Smith. *Serpentine*. Truro: Truran, 2005.

Scolding, Bill. *Five Walks Around Mount Edgcumbe and the Rame Peninsula*. Cornwall County Council 2007.

Sotnick, Richard. *The Coburg Conspiracy: Victoria and Albert – Royal Plots and Manoeuvres*. Great Britain: Ephesus Publishing, 2010.

St Aubyn, Giles. *Edward VII: Prince and King*. London: William Collins Sons & Co Ltd 1979.

St Aubyn, James. *A Personal Tour of St Michael's Mount*. James and Mary St Aubyn, 2010.

St Aubyn, John. *St Michael's Mount: Illustrated History and Guide*. John St Aubyn, 1978.

Tait, Derek. *Rame Peninsula Through Time*. Stroud: Amberley Publishing, 2010.

The Life and Times of Queen Victoria. London: Cassell and Company, 1901.

Turner, Michael. *Osborne*. London: English Heritage, 2007.

Victoria, Queen of Great Britain and Ireland. *Queen Victoria's Journals*. www.queenvictoriasjournals.org

Weir, Alison. *Richard III and The Princes in The Tower*. London: Vintage Books, 2014.

Whitwell Wilson, Philip (edited). *The Greville Diary: Including Pages Hitherto Withheld from Publication*. New York: Doubleday Page & Company, 1927.

Woodham-Smith, Cecil. *Queen Victoria Her Life and Times: Volume I, 1819 – 1861*. London: Hamish Hamilton, 1972.

Wreyford, Paul. *The Little History of Cornwall*. Stroud: The History Press, 2018.

Queen Victoria has a life story that is full of drama, intrigue, and surprises. She is the British monarch in history whose name everyone knows. Susan Symon's series of books focus on the queen as a woman – her personal life, events that formed her resolute character, and relationships that were important to her. They are illustrated throughout with portraits and memorabilia from the author's collection and use some of Victoria's own words, from her letters and journal, to help tell the story.

If you thought history was dull, this author will make you think again.
Roseland Arts Festival.

Young Victoria covers the bizarre events of Victoria's birth, when there was a scramble to produce the next heir to the throne; her lonely childhood under a tough regime; and the national adulation when she came to the throne aged eighteen. *Victoria & Albert* tells the story of one of the most famous relationships in history. There were early troubles with a personality clash and struggle for dominance in the relationship. They came through these to create a true partnership and found a dynasty.

The style is lively and the illustrations gorgeous. I highly recommend this book!
Amazon review.

SUSAN SYMONS

Victoria the Widowed Queen

THE COLOURFUL PERSONAL LIFE OF
QUEEN VICTORIA ~ PART 3

Victoria the Widowed Queen covers the long years of Victoria's widowhood when she became an icon of the age and matriarch of a huge clan. The first years as a widow were the least successful of her reign. She refused to appear in public and her popularity suffered. She gradually emerged from gloom but her seclusion in remote homes fuelled rumours about her private life. Her relationship with a servant caused scandal and later in life she had a puzzling relationship with a young Indian man.

Susan is on a mission to promote royal history to as many readers as possible.
Royalty Digest Quarterly Journal

SUSAN SYMONS

Victoria's Daughters

THE COLOURFUL PERSONAL LIFE OF
QUEEN VICTORIA ~ PART 4

Coming next: *Victoria's Daughters* explores the stories of her five daughters, tinged with tragedy and scandal. Victoria had qualities that made her a great queen, but she was not at her best as a mother. The princesses were born into privilege and deference. But their lives were blighted by the early death of their father, Prince Albert, and dominated by the demands of their controlling mother. Her daughters were important public figures in their own time but are largely forgotten today.

Susan has done another fantastic job, proving that history can also be fun...
Eurohistory: The European Royal History Journal

Schloss is the German word for castle or palace, and you are never far from one of these in Germany. For most of its history Germany was not a single country but a patchwork of royal states, held together under the banner of the Holy Roman Empire. The dukes and princes who ruled these states were passionate builders. Their beautiful castles and palaces, and their compelling personal stories, provide the material for the *Schloss* series of books.

This book can be seen as an inspiration ... to get out there and find the lesser known palaces and learn more about their history.
Royalty Digest Quarterly Journal.

Each of the *Schloss* books includes twenty-five beautiful castles and palaces in Germany and looks at these from two perspectives. The first is the author's experience as an overseas visitor to each schloss; the second, colourful stories of the historical royal families connected with them. Royalty have always been the celebrities of their day, and these stories from history can rival anything in modern-day television soap operas.

The second volume is as good as the first, maybe even better – a must...
Amazon review.

The stories in the *Schloss* books include the mistress of the king who tried to blackmail him and was imprisoned for forty-nine years; the princess from a tiny German state who used her body and her brains to become the ruler of the vast Russian empire; the prince who defied his family to marry a pharmacist's daughter and then bought her the rank of royal princess; and the duke whose personal story is so colourful he has been called the Bavarian Henry VIII!

The author's indefatigable enthusiam shines out from each page. I am loving this series ...
Amazon review.

The German princes abdicated in 1918, at the end of World War I, and Germany became a republic. As they lost their royal families, many castles and palaces went into decline and became prisons, workhouses, and other institutions. Some were damaged or destroyed in World War II; others lay behind the Iron Curtain for fifty years. The books chart these difficult years and their resurgence and use today as public buildings, museums, and hotels.

The latest addition visits Bavaria – and what a treat it is. Fascinating reading!
The European Royal History Journal

THE SCHLOSS SERIES OF BOOKS

The castles and palaces in the books range in time from fortified castles of the middle-ages; to grand palaces built in imitation of Louis XIV's Versailles; to stately homes from the turn of the early twentieth century. Many are not well known outside Germany and some rarely see an English-speaking visitor. The *Schloss* books might encourage you to go and see these wonderful places for yourself.

The books are sympathetic to our fascinating German royal history and make linkages and connections in a clear and interesting way.
European Castles Institute, Schloss Philippsburg, Germany.

The *Schloss* books are intended to be light-hearted and easy to read. Illustrated throughout and supplemented with charts and family trees, they should appeal to anyone who likes history or sightseeing or is interested in people's personal stories. With dozens of royal families in Germany before the monarchy fell, there are still many more castles and palaces to go, and Susan is already at work on the next book.

This is a well-written, entertaining display of the castles ... I am definitely off to Thuringia, Symons' book in hand.
Royalty Digest Quarterly Journal

Printed in Great Britain
by Amazon

81925320R00102